A Touch of Glory

It's Your Destiny

Lindell Cooley

Revival Press

An Imprint of
Destiny Image® **Publishers, Inc.**
P.O. Box 310
Shippensburg, PA 17257-0310

ISBN 1-56043-689-1

For Worldwide Distribution
Printed in the U.S.A.

First Printing: 1997   Second Printing: 1997

This book and all other Destiny Image, Revival Press, and Treasure House books are available at Christian bookstores and distributors worldwide.

For a U.S. bookstore nearest you, call **1-800-722-6774**. For more information on foreign distributors, call **717-532-3040**.
Or reach us on the Internet: **http://www.reapernet.com**

Check out the Brownsville website:
http://www.brownsville-revival.org

Dedication

I dedicate this book to my greatest mentors,
Gene and Shirley Cooley

Contents

Foreword

Back in 1985, I had Rusty Goodman come to Brownsville Assembly of God Church for ministry. He brought with him a 23-year-old pastor's son from Red Bay, Alabama. That pastor's son was Lindell Cooley. Some musicians are musicians—but this young man had a heart. He wept uncontrollably as our choir sang an old hymn. My heart bonded with Lindell's right then. Although 10 years would pass before Lindell would join my staff, still I never forgot him. God had to put Lindell Cooley on the potter's wheel to make him what he is today. God shaped and molded him through life's experiences. As I have often said, "Everything is Father filtered." God made the man, but then He had to put him in the fire to test him. Bred into this psalmist is more than just a Pentecostal heritage—he carries in his soul the echoes of the Church of yesteryear and the sounds of tomorrow.

A Touch of Glory will let you take a candid and biographical look into the life of one of America's most loved psalmists.

I'm glad Shirley Cooley prayed that, if God would give her a son, then she would give him to God to use. As you read *A Touch of Glory*, you will come to the same conclusion I have: God isn't through with this man of God; there's much more locked up in his soul than even Lindell knows is in there. You'll be hearing much more from the pastor's son from Red Bay, Alabama.

John A. Kilpatrick, Pastor
Brownsville Assembly of God Church

Introduction

When God sovereignly sends revival to a people, He always intends for the fire to spread beyond that place and people. Leaders across the world agree that God is raising up an army of "unknowns" around the world who will take the gospel of Jesus Christ to every nation with anointing and power. It is a Bible precedent that obscure people like shepherds, fishermen, and residents in forgotten places like Bethlehem and Red Bay, Alabama (where my parents live), be raised up for world-changing tasks. Why? I believe at least one reason is that God then receives all the glory. He does not have to share it with proud flesh and inflated human egos as long as the humble men and women He chooses remember "whence cometh their help" (see Ps. 121:1).

This book was written for the countless "unknowns" who, like me and many others across the world, are being plucked from obscurity for a divine work of destiny.

If you have picked up this book hoping to find a formula or methodoligical key to revival, then you are going to be sorely disappointed. Formulas and methods have absolutely nothing to do with true revival. God alone is the author of revival—methods seem to be immaterial to His work. The Holy Spirit has operated equally powerfully through the radically different methods employed by the formerly unknown leaders in Argentina, at the Toronto Airport Christian Fellowship in Ontario, Canada, at Trinity Brompton Anglican Church in London, and at Brownsville Assembly of God in Pensacola, Florida. God is unruffled and unhindered by differences in culture, language, theology, and ministry styles because they have nothing to do with revival—He alone is the Key.

Yet there are some important similarities. The most important key in these revivals centers on a life-changing encounter with the presence of the living God. Anointed, uninhibited worship also plays a key role in virtually every revival. Unabashed hunger for more of God is another trademark. Finally, in every place where the fires of revival have ignited, God's people have sensed a new passion for winning the lost to their Savior. As a result, hundreds of thousands are coming to Christ each year!

Everything about my life has to do with God's grace, with my parents' sacrifices, and with God's eternal plan. There is no room for pride or boasting on my part. All I know is that I am blessed to be a child of

God who is playing a part in the great revival in Pensacola, Florida, today. My prayer is that this book will help ignite the fire of revival in your own life, and lead you to a personal and up-close encounter with the living God.

There is no substitute for His touch of glory. I must warn you: Once you taste and see that the Lord is good, there is no turning back. Nothing else will do. From that moment onward you will live by an eternal standard of joy and fulfillment that cannot be satisfied outside of God's abiding presence. It is a wonderful way to live, but it is not a path for cowards or pretenders. If you long for a touch of God's glory, you need only voice the cry of your hungry heart. God will move Heaven and hell to meet you where you are at, with joy unspeakable and full of glory.

Chapter 1

Touched by Glory, Brushed by Death

The young woman standing beside the window was only 22, and resigned to a childless life. As she glanced across Florissant Street from her south-side apartment in St. Louis, Missouri, she saw a woman walking toward a tavern with her twins in a stroller. Her heart broke when she saw the mother disappear through the tavern door with her twins in tow. She wiped away a tear and looked upward past the rooftops as she thought of the two children she had lost in pregnancy—one at only three months, and the second in a tragic stillborn birth two and a half years earlier.

She was unaware that her baby was dead at the time because, according to her doctors, she had also died on the operating table during delivery. After all hope was gone, the teenage mother was declared dead; but she shocked her doctors by suddenly reviving on the table. When she remained unconscious in a vegetative coma for eight consecutive days, the doctors felt that their patient had lost so much blood during the ordeal that she had suffered irreversible brain damage.

The senior physician reluctantly told the woman's young husband that his wife would never again hear his voice, see the light of day, speak, walk, or care for herself. She had proved them wrong on every count, but she could still hear the doctor's devastating statement that she would never bear children after the stillbirth. She had resigned herself to her lot in life until the moment she looked out of her window on that fateful morning.

With her eyes now fixed on the battered door of the tavern, the young woman's thoughts turned to her husband. She longed with all her heart to give him a child, a legacy of the godliness he had exhibited every day they had been together. Her heart cried out in silent prayer, "Dear heavenly Father, would You give me a child? The doctors say I'll never have children, but they don't know about Your power."

As the tears began to flow, the young woman's passion burst through her pain as she uttered a desperate prayer in the tradition of Hannah of old: "Lord, if I had a baby I wouldn't take him any place like that. Jesus, if You'll give me a child, I'll raise him and train him to Your purpose." That very moment she felt the glory of God overshadow and engulf her body, and she knew that God had totally healed her. Then the Lord assured her that she would have a baby, but she didn't say anything to anyone about it. She hid these things in her heart.

Four months later, this young woman couldn't shake the persistent nausea that was plaguing her, so she went to the doctor. With a puzzled look on his face, he told his young patient, "Mrs. Cooley, you're not sick—you are four months pregnant." Five months later in 1963, a baby boy entered the world without any complications. His mother and father named their miracle son "Lindell." Two weeks later he was dedicated to the Lord in a Pentecostal revival meeting.

The first time I heard my mother share this story about her "Hannah prayer" was during a phone conversation while I was writing this book. The moment I heard my mother share this story between her sobs and tears, I knew I had found the beginning of the book. The proper focus is not upon me, but upon the living God who ordained and orchestrated my miraculous birth. I firmly believe that no one enters this world by accident, regardless of the circumstances of his or her conception or delivery. Yet there are also cases where God prepares people from the womb for specific tasks. Either way, whether the preparation comes early or late, when men and women are obedient, God receives all the glory.

From the very beginning, my mother prayed over my hands and dedicated them to the glory of God. More than three decades after my mother made her heartbroken plea to God, and after years of faithful prayer over my hands, I am leading thousands of hungry people into the presence of God seven and eight times a week in a miraculous revival of almost unprecedented proportions in the United States. Nearly every week I stop to marvel at how God has brought me step by step from a heartbroken "Hannah's prayer" in

St. Louis almost four decades ago to the incredible Brownsville Revival today. The answer is clear:

> *But God hath chosen the foolish things of the world to confound the wise; and God hath chosen the weak things of the world to confound the things which are mighty; and base things of the world, and things which are despised, hath God chosen, yea, and **things which are not**, to bring to nought things that are: that no flesh should glory in His presence* (1 Corinthians 1:27-29).

Week after week, I see thousands of hungry souls stream forward to the altars in our revival services at Brownsville Assembly of God Church in Pensacola, Florida. Many come forward to repent of their sins and receive Jesus Christ as Lord for the very first time in their lives. Many others come to repent of their sins and renew their commitment to Christ, or to receive healing for an inner wound or physical infirmity. Some receive miraculous deliverances from demonic oppression or possession through the blood of the Lamb. A large number simply come forward for "more of God." Nearly all come to the revival just hoping that *what they have heard about the revival is really true.* They want more of God.

I believe history will mark the Brownsville Revival as the beginning of one of the greatest moves of God in modern history. Well over 1.5 million people have streamed to little Pensacola from every sector of this planet, and more than 100,000 have received

Jesus Christ as Lord and Savior in only two years' time. Multiplied thousands of believers and ministers of the gospel have left Brownsville Assembly of God with fresh fire for the work of God. Revival has spread across the globe from Pensacola, Toronto, and many other key places in the world. Only God can track all of the good fruit borne by this revival of holiness and dedication to His purposes.

I've noticed that my life has been marked by *touches of glory* from the very first visitation on my mother's womb. By "glory" I refer to God's overpowering, overwhelming presence. Each time God touched me, major transformations took place in my nature and prepared me to fulfill a destiny that only God could fully perceive. Pastor John Kilpatrick explains that the Hebrew word for glory is *kabod*. It literally means "weightiness." Whereas the *anointing* of God is "a supernatural enablement from God to accomplish His purposes," the *glory* is the manifestation of His weighty and awe-inspiring presence upon an individual or corporate body. It is as if God enters a room, and suddenly there isn't enough space for anyone else. In the presence of God's glory, we become keenly sensitive to our conspicuous sin and shortcomings in comparison to His weighty holiness and power.

Encountering the Glory

When you encounter God's glory, you have no doubts about His existence or His ability to intervene in human affairs. Every thought of debating or arguing with Him vanishes. At one moment you almost feel undone by the stark contrast between your sinfulness and His utter holiness. In the next moment you are engulfed in unspeakable ecstasy and totally lost in wonder at the Creator who has chosen to love you so persistently and unconditionally. One thing is almost universal: You won't act as if everything is normal. Every time God's glory has fallen upon me, I have wept openly, unashamedly, and usually uncontrollably. Others collapse under the weight of His glory, and their overburdened nervous systems often trigger inexplicable tremors or shaking of the limbs, which usually persist until God's glory lifts from the individual.

With that brief explanation, I want to describe the sovereign ways in which God shaped and prepared me for my destiny (as much as I can see at this point). Again I share these things not to glorify myself or my family, but to demonstrate the marvelous way in which God works in individual lives to accomplish His purposes. When you lay down this book, I pray that you will glorify God for His wisdom and majesty rather than say, "My, but that Lindell Cooley is such a wonderful guy." No, Lindell Cooley is a redeemed and blessed guy who is very, very thankful for God's mercy, grace, and guidance each day. It is only by God's grace that I have anything to share with you today! If anything, this book should encourage you. I hope it inspires comments like, "Well, if God could use Lindell Cooley like that, then He can surely use me!"

Four months after I was born, my mother was rocking me to sleep and praying over my hands as usual. As she kissed my fingers, Mom prayed, "Jesus, use these hands. Lord, anoint these hands. He is Yours; I give him totally to You for Your use." Then the Lord spoke to her and said, "What you give to Me, I will take." The Lord let her know right then that my hands were anointed. I didn't know this either until that recent phone call, but my mother asked God to anoint me to play the piano. Now I was never interested in the piano as a kid. I just wanted to play the drums, which I did. It is obvious that I did ultimately learn how to play the piano, but it all began with a mother's prayer.

Just five months later, at the age of nine months, the enemy made his first attempt on my life. Every month that my mother carried me in her womb, she battled a nagging fear that something would happen to me, just as it had to my unborn siblings. Nine months after my birth, I suddenly developed a high fever while Dad was at work, and the devil began to tell my mother that I was going to die. This fever was dangerously high, and nothing would make it go down. When satan continued to torment her, my mother began to pray. She prayed for me all night long and finally dozed off to sleep just before dawn. Then my mother felt somebody touch her shoulder and a voice said, "Turn over." When she looked over toward my crib, she was shaken by the sight of angels hovering over me. Then the Lord spoke to her and said, "Don't fear. Your son is in My hands. I have My hand on him and the devil can't take him." She told me that she has had to remind the devil of that several times.

The enemy made a second major attack on me on Halloween night in my seventh year. My family was always in a revival on Halloween night while the other kids went trick or treating. I remember that I cried and begged my parents to stay home from church that night so I could go trick or treating too. My dad said, "No sir, this is church night and you're going to church." I even told my mother that Jesus wouldn't care, but it didn't do any good. I went to church. (All the kids from church who stayed home and made the trick or treat rounds gave me a big grocery bag full of candy that they had collected, so I didn't miss out on any cavity activity.)

I was the church drummer by that time, so I went to sit by the drums. When my mother looked at me, she immediately noticed that my eyes had crossed. All I can remember is that I kept blinking my eyes and shaking my head. I knew something was wrong because my eyes just wouldn't focus together like they were supposed to. Mom and Dad ran over to me along with the pastor and they began to pray for me. In less than two minutes, my eyes straightened up perfectly. The devil is a liar, isn't he?

The third demonic attack on my life came in my tenth year on the day after I had experienced another touch of God's glory during a revival service. I was ten years old, and we had just moved from St. Louis to a small town in Alabama. The night before, on Friday night, my father's church had a revival service. Before the night was over, I ended up at the altar with two friends who were my age, and we were all deeply touched by the Lord and were speaking in tongues. The next day was Saturday and I went to help these boys harvest watermelons with their grandfather.

All day long we picked up those huge watermelons and loaded them onto a wagon, and it was hard work—especially for ten-year-old boys. By the end of the day we had loaded approximately 2,000 pounds worth of watermelons onto the produce wagon attached to the grandfather's tractor. We decided to go back in for the evening and the other boys (the two friends from church plus a third friend) piled onto the tractor driven by their grandfather.

The tractor was already moving slowly, and like everybody else, I jumped up toward the drawbar where the wagon tongue attached to the tractor chassis. Unfortunately I lost my footing and I fell right under the produce wagon. The wheels of the wagon ran over the entire left side of my body and my head. I know the wheels passed over my head because I can still remember watching the first tire treads as it bounced right over my head. If you were to draw a line from my forehead down across my nose and then straight down to the spot between my feet, you would have a good idea of where that tire went.

My friends and their grandfather had to carry me in from the field because I was unconscious. When they brought me into the house, my mother didn't run to grab me. She ran to the bedroom and fell on her knees instead. She began to pray from the depths of her soul, "Lord, he belongs to You. And You said You were going to use him. I still remember that promise from when Lindell was only four and a half months old, and *it still hasn't come to pass*, Lord. Jesus, he's in Your hands." Then she hurried out and joined the others as they rushed me to the hospital, still unconscious.

Everyone who saw the accident went with me to the hospital, and they were worried. The accident was horrible to watch, and the weight of that loaded wagon was so great that when the tires ran along the length of my body, they literally unbuttoned all my clothes and ripped them to shreds. You can imagine their astonishment when the doctors came out and said that their x-rays showed there was nothing wrong with me! There were no broken bones or signs of a concussion, so they sent me home.

I still remember being so sore that I couldn't sleep or walk. My mother wasn't finished yet. She put me in a recliner in the living room and then she started hunting for Bibles. She put one Bible under my feet, another one under my back, and a third Bible under my head. Then Mom and Dad prayed for me and went to bed. Somehow I slept in the chair, and the next morning I woke Mom up at six o'clock wanting breakfast. I was standing at the foot of her bed, and when we walked to the kitchen I had no limp. I can still remember that like it just happened yesterday.

I am sharing these experiences to make one point: I was introduced to the glory of the Lord at a very early age. The glory of God is something you never forget. Once you are engulfed and carried away in His presence, nothing else will do. You can't be fooled or beguiled because nothing compares with God's glory. I can always tell if someone knows the glory or not—somehow it just shows up in the way you walk, talk, and live. The glory will mark you as a separated, called-out person. Whether you are prepared to accept it or not, the truth is that once you experience the glory of God, you will be changed.

God's Glory Touched My Family

The night I received the baptism in the Holy Spirit was a night when God's glory touched our family during a revival and literally saved my mother's life. For years before that revival, I had often played church like kids will do. I used to preach the sermons, lead the songs, and dance before the Lord while doing my own "do-it-yourself" version of speaking in other tongues. (I was a Pentecostal preacher's kid, so it was natural.)

This revival was held in Mt. View, Missouri. None of us knew it, but my mother was suffering from what must have been an advanced case of breast cancer at that time. Our old family friend, Evangelist E.R. Wright, was completing a 21-day fast when the Lord told him to go to Mt. View, Missouri, immediately. When he arrived, my mother was so sick that she couldn't stay up to do her work, so my father's mother was doing her housework for her. This had been going on for about six months, and she was obviously getting worse.

Brother Wright looked at my mother and said, "I came here because the Lord spoke to me and said, 'If Shirley Cooley doesn't receive a miracle, she will not be living very long.'" Then he looked up and told everyone there, "She is going to receive a miracle from the Lord tonight. I want to pray for her." When the evangelist laid his hands on my mother, she told us later that she felt an intense burning sensation in her chest, her lungs, and in the upper half of her body. She was laid out on the floor in the Spirit for about two hours. When she got up, she was healed. Her strength had been completely restored, and she never had another problem.

That night at the revival, an invitation was given for anyone who wanted to receive the Holy Spirit, so I went forward. After I was prayed for, I spoke in other tongues and cried for almost two hours. As the revival continued that week, I was visited by the Lord so powerfully that my parents had to lift me off the floor and carry me home—and I was speaking in tongues and crying the whole way. When they got me home, I was still speaking in tongues, and it just kept on going after they put me in bed. (It sounds kind of like revival today, doesn't it? It should—the same God inspired them both.)

My early encounters with the living God set high standards for holiness and truth that have helped me in every area of life since then. His glory will do the same in your life. Another reason I will share much of my testimony in this book is to show God's determination to mold an imperfect vessel with low self-esteem into a vessel fit for His purposes. This imperfect vessel can assure you that God is out to conform you to the image of His Son too.

Chapter 2

The Doubting Minstrel

Too many Christians look at successful people in the Church and think to themselves, *My, but that man is blessed of God. His incredible abilities have brought him far. Lord, I'd like to have the skills and training that guy has.* The truth is that nothing and no one other than Jesus Christ is perfect. I owe everything that is good in my life to my merciful God. Most of the time, the only things that I added to my life's equation were confusion and weakness.

The truth is that I was a very insecure, overweight little Pentecostal preacher's boy who never thought much of myself. It is only in recent years that I have been able to bring my weight under control. My self-consciousness about my obesity dominated me from my childhood. Most people are shocked when they hear this, but anyone who knew me in the past can testify to it.

Joy in the Church

My greatest assets and positive memories from childhood all center around the church, the ministry, music, and the family. Through all those years I can remember my joy in going to church. I loved it. I was an odd duck, I suppose. Every Sunday night, "The Walt Disney Show" would come on and I never got to watch it. I used to think that Tinkerbell the fairy's flying through the air and waving her wand was my personal signal that it was about time to go to church on Sunday night. That was the most I ever saw of the Disney show, and I saw even less of other programs.

From time to time, my wife Amber will ask me if I've seen a certain episode of those early TV classics, and when I shake my head no, she always seems astonished. "Do you mean that you've never seen that? It is impossible for anyone to *not* know about Charlie Brown, Lucy, Schroeder, Sally, Peppermint Patty, and Marci? Surely you know about Linus, 'the little red-haired girl,' and Snoopy and Woodstock?" (I think she had to think twice about marrying me when she learned about my "deprived" childhood.)

I never thought of myself as a deprived child because church was always a joy for me. My parents weren't militant about church attendance—they were loving about it. I just grew up knowing that we were going to go to church. According to my father, you had to be close to death to not go to church. My parents even took me to church when I had a fever, and I imagine a lot of people today would consider that child abuse.

Most Christian parents today would say, "Oh, my baby's sick. We'll just stay home." My parents looked at it from a totally different perspective. They would say, "Let's get our baby up and get him to church. God will heal him." Do you know what? Almost every time they were right! Nearly every time I went to church with a fever and chills—even the times I went to church when I was throwing up every five minutes—I would only get halfway through the service before the Lord would touch me. This was a living and graphic illustration of the godly faith of my parents. I stayed home the times I caught the measles and the whooping cough (pertussis), but that was about it. I guess my parents didn't want to risk my passing along these diseases to another child between the time I arrived at church and the time God healed me.

I don't understand what has changed. God is still God and His Word is still true. I suppose we are the ones who have changed. I am in no position to judge others, but I do know that my parents' faith in God's ability and willingness to heal instilled a strong belief in me that God would heal. It made me a soldier in a lot of ways. I could never hold up under this continuous revival schedule if I hadn't had that training in faithfulness as a young child.

There are some nights when I honestly don't feel like going to revival services. Sometimes I begin to feel physically sick when five o'clock rolls around, but I also know it's not God. It is just a wave of fatigue, mental tiredness, stress, or outright devilish interference trying to overtake me. That is when the soldier in me rises up and declares, "Honey, I've got to get ready. I don't want to go, and I sure don't feel like going, but I need to take a shower, load everything in the car, and be there on time. I've got a feeling that the Lord is going to visit us in power tonight." Every time I deny my flesh and step up to the battle line, the joy of God's presence sweeps in to give new strength, power, and compassion for the hungry people who have come to meet with God. I still love to go to church, even though I am in long revival services at least five times a week throughout most of the year.

God Put Discerning People in My Life

God allowed a number of godly people to see the potential He had placed in me, and they were encouraging me and prodding me to develop it long before I ever saw or acknowledged any talent or calling in my life.

I especially remember the evangelist who first prophesied over me during a tent revival when I was four and a half years old. His name was E.R. Wright, and he was from Lafayette, Louisiana. Before he was saved, he was a drug dealer, an addict and alcoholic, and a pimp who owned houses of prostitution. When he received Christ, he began to tear up the devil's kingdom with bold preaching and signs and wonders. Later in his life he was diagnosed with prostate cancer but the Lord miraculously healed him of that. He was the first to declare this word of the Lord over my life:

You will be blessed in music and you will stand before thousands and thousands of people. You will play an instrument and as you play, your music will be so anointed that people will be healed and delivered. Your ministry will be so great that your parents will stand back in disbelief and awe. And then your music will go to the nations.

I can still remember feeling God's presence so strongly that night that I cried and cried and cried. I get really concerned and burdened when I look at all the little kids in our services and in the churches I visit. I want them to experience the presence of God like I did. It changes you somehow, and I want every one of them to know what it's like. Sure, I was still a kid in every other aspect after my experience, but I felt this "debt" or obligation to God that I just couldn't sway. The glory of the Lord brings unspeakable joy, but it carries a sense of heaviness too. When you experience the glory of God, it somehow plants a new perspective of life inside you. It is like Heaven's brand is burned into your inner being. These encounters with the glory of the Lord happened over and over in my life.

From time to time, that same prophecy would resurface but through the lips of a totally different evangelist or pastor who was led to lay hands on me and prophesy. It is ironic that in those early days, I didn't even play an instrument. These men of God hadn't seen me playing an instrument or doing astounding musical feats that would lead them to say the things they said. They had to speak it out by sheer faith because the only thing I had back then was rhythm.

My parents were my first and greatest mentors, of course, but God sent along many others besides. I preached my first sermon at the ripe old age of five because of my Uncle James Gardner. Uncle James was a pastor who helped a lot of young ministers get their start in the ministry. I didn't understand Uncle James back then, but he knew that the glory of God was on me. When I was only five years old he asked me to prepare a sermon, and I did. It was very simple, of course. I can't remember what it was about, but I do remember that it was really short. It must have lasted a whole minute or two, but Uncle James saw the glory of God in me from the very beginning and he wanted to see it developed and cultivated even then. I praise God for him today, and I'm determined to follow in his footsteps. Whenever I see young people with the glory on them, I want to help them get started too.

I believe that any of us who are following the Lord can look back in our lives and see a pattern of divine appointments scattered throughout our past. From the very beginning, the glory of the Lord was following me, and prophetic words continually declared and confirmed a greater plan for my life in one way or another. It began with the "Hannah's prayer" my mother prayed in St. Louis, but that was just the tip of the iceberg.

One of the reasons I enjoyed church so much as a child was because I really met God in those services. I remember that I would always weep a lot when the Spirit of the Lord would touch me. I can remember many nights at our lively little Pentecostal church when I would grab a tambourine and dance before the Lord as a little boy. Of course there were times when it wasn't motivated by God, but then there were times when it was *all* God. I haven't talked about this much with other people, but I know that the Lord wants me to share it in this book for some reason.

Despite all the protests and arguments you might hear to the contrary, *there is a dance that is holy unto the Lord.* Over the years I have become inhibited, perhaps due to my age, or due to the fear of what people might think. Yet I tell you that there are times during the revival meetings at Brownsville when I feel the glory of God coming on me for the *dance* that is holy unto the Lord. It is perfectly acceptable to dance for joy before the Lord when you hear an anointed song and to praise the Lord in dance, but this dance of the Spirit is different.

There were times when I was a little boy when I would be literally caught up in the presence of the Lord! I felt like I entered another world, a holy world, a set-apart world where God alone received praise. When this glory fell on me as a little boy, I could dance for hours in the Spirit.

Many times I would wake up on the floor, and the back of my head was usually wet because of the flood of tears that flowed from my eyes down my cheeks and into my ears and hair. I didn't know it then, but I was experiencing the glory of God in those years. I pray that I will once again dare to be so uninhibited before my King. I believe that He is about to bring the holy dance back into the Church, the kind of dance that caused King David to dance and leap and whirl with all his might as he led the people in a procession of joy before the presence of God represented by the ark of the covenant (see 2 Sam. 6).

The Glory of God Always Irritates the Critics

As I recall, my childhood experiences with the glory of God met with mixed reactions in our Pentecostal church. Some people told my mother, "Now why do you let your child do that? He's only six. He doesn't even know what he is doing." Then others said everything from "That's cute," to "That is really the glory of the Lord on Lindell. Don't you bother him. Just leave him alone—that's God."

Those days are vividly stored in my memory. Even now as I write about those times, I can feel the presence of the Lord. I don't talk about it much, and before I began writing this book, I hadn't even shared it with my wife. Now the truth is known. Let those with ears to hear...

My very first memories as a child are of church services in St. Louis. On Friday and Saturday nights, we ministered in an African-American church, and on Sunday mornings and the rest of the time we would be in a white church. My parents were always working as choir directors or song leaders. My dad was working a secular job then (and running from God's call to full-time ministry), but on his day off he would go out on Saturdays and knock on doors in North St. Louis so he could fill up his car with visitors and make three trips to get people to church on Sunday. The interdenominational Pentecostal church where my parents worked was in downtown St. Louis, before all the churches evacuated from the inner city.

Music came naturally for me because every week I saw my mom playing organ and my father serving as a song leader. My parents also used to work with tent preachers and other pastors. In fact, my first memory of music dates back to a tent meeting in Wilmington, Delaware. I was four or five years old then. I do remember that it was a big tent. My parents have told me it held four or five thousand people, and about 4800 of those folks were African-Americans. I remember that my mom played this big Hammond B3, and we had three or four African-American ladies who sang backup and played tambourine. Basically, it was what we would call a worship team today. I learned to play tambourine from those ladies who worked with my parents. At times I feel the glory of the Lord on me to get my tambourine and dance before the Lord in a holy war dance.

I loved music from the very beginning. I started playing drums when I was five or six, but I didn't play

them in the church in those days. I can still remember
my father going out to buy me my first set of drums
with his income tax check. He paid $90 for the set, and
I played those drums until I was 12 or 13 years old.

The Misery of Running From the Call

I'll never forget the day that my father left St. Louis.
We actually lived in Crystal City, Missouri, at the time,
and Dad finally accepted the call to preach. His running from the call nearly killed us because we were
starving to death. He had a union job with the American Can Company, and the pay was good. The only
problem was that he didn't have enough seniority to
keep from being laid off. He would work three months
and be laid off for six, so we had tough times. We did
really well when he was working, and really bad when
he wasn't. Things finally got so bad that Dad moved us
to Popular Bluff, Missouri, so my mother could be
around her mother and father and her sisters.

During the three or four months he wasn't laid off,
he would drive to St. Louis where he would stay and
work during the week and then come home on weekends. When he was off, he lived with us. This went on
for awhile, and during these "off" times Dad would
stay busy doing the church work he loved so much.
Dad was always sincere about the Lord (and he still is),
but finally he told me and Mother, "I'm going to accept the call."

We usually traveled and ministered on weekends,
and Dad would always preach his one and only sermon

in those days, "If ye abide in Me, and My words abide in you" (see Jn. 15:7). He preached that wherever we went. By that time, we were singing together as a family too.

Then we heard about a little church in Alabama that needed a pastor. My uncle was the district superintendent overseeing this church, and he told Dad, "Look, they need somebody to come down and just run a revival while they are in this interim period." So we went down to this tiny church on a Sunday and held a morning service. There were only 30 people there. I remember riding through town after church when my parents were looking for a place to eat. To a kid from St. Louis, Red Bay looked like a ghost town. There was nothing there. There weren't even any cars there. I looked at my dad and said, "Is this a ghost town? Is everybody dead? Dad, I hate this place. I don't want to be here. This place is pitiful. It is the pits. I don't want to be here." I remember telling my father, "Dad, please don't stay."

So we did the revival and the people really loved us. We had just returned to the Crystal City suburbs, about 30 miles south of St. Louis, when my uncle called back and said, "These people really want you to consider taking this church to pastor." On that same day, my dad got a call from the American Can Company. They said, "You have just been lifted in seniority. No more layoffs will affect you. If you will stay with this company, you will get 16 weeks of paid vacation. If you will stay here for ten years or more, then you will build up even more paid vacation time." Basically, they were telling Dad he would never be fired.

Despite the tempting offer, Dad kept his word to the Lord and took the leap of faith. The entire Cooley family packed up and headed to Alabama to pastor that church in the middle of nowhere. We soon found out that the church had a bad name and that it was a "one family" church (which means one family controlled the church government and supplied most of the finances).

After a year had passed, the ruling family decided they didn't like what Dad was preaching. They didn't appreciate his strong stand on God's Word when he said, "If you don't pay tithes, you're not going to teach Sunday school. If you don't pay tithes, then you are not faithful and you are not going to be a deacon or usher." Dad had worked hard over the last 12 months, and he had nearly doubled the original attendance of 30. He was learning how hard it is to overcome a bad name in a little town of about 3,000 people.

To make a long story short, the "family" wanted to throw Dad out of the church. I heard very little of this because my parents didn't believe in talking about that kind of thing, but there was a business meeting and things turned nasty.

Incidentally, the organ that my dad bought while he was at that church was probably one of the things that spurred me on to be a musician. I would go there and play it even though I didn't know anything about playing it. This Hammond organ sounded good, and it also had percussion and drums and all kinds of bells and whistles on it.

The business meeting occurred on a Saturday evening and the next morning when we got ready to go to church, I noticed that my parents didn't say much. I remember my mother saying, "Well, Gene, are we leaving?" My Dad stopped in the doorway as we were leaving and said, "I don't know." Dad stepped behind the pulpit that morning and conducted the service, and at the end he said, "Yesterday we had a business meeting, and I have to say quite honestly that I didn't come here to split the church. However, there are about 25 or 30 of you people who don't want to miss God, and you don't want the same old garbage." As he looked across the congregation, he said, "I can't leave you. Next Sunday we'll have church someplace else if we have to."

Seventy-five to 80 people showed up for the first service of the new congregation on that first Sunday. My dad has been there 25 years, and although his church still wouldn't qualify as a "big" church, it is nevertheless a successful church. All his critics in the first church are dead and gone. Dad literally outlived his critics. I often felt the glory fall on me in that old church, and as I relive it for you in these pages, it is all coming alive again. These are my spiritual roots of what some call "old Pentecost," and they are very dear to my heart.

I Received a Life-Changing Vision

At the age of 14, I started playing bass guitar, organ, and piano. I had a strong sense of destiny in my life because of the many prophecies spoken over me. I knew it was going to happen but I never felt cocky about it. It was during this time that I received a vision from the Lord during a Sunday night service. I remember going to the altar and kneeling down with a tremendous burden. I just buried my face in my arms and cried for a long time. It was during this time that I had what could only have been a vision. I saw an audio mixing console with fader bars or sliding volume controls, and superimposed over it I saw the VU-meters of a multitrack tape recorder. Well, I had never seen a mixing console before. The most advanced piece of equipment at our church was our little Shure VocalMaster amplifier/mixer. To my knowledge, there was no such thing as a console with slider bars in those days. Nearly ever audio recording board was still using "rotary pots" or rotating knobs to control volume and equalization adjustments.

When I saw this vision of a recording console with all those slider bars, I didn't know what it was but I knew it had to do with music. On top of all that, I saw the image of a cassette tape, and that really confused me because cassette tapes just weren't as familiar then as they are today. The Lord said to me at that point, "I want to use you to take music around the world." I thought to myself, *Lord, I'm in Alabama. I'm in a one-horse town. What do You mean by telling me to take music around the world?*

Despite my questions, the presence of the Lord so moved me that I told Him, "Lord, whatever You want me to do, just open the doors and I'll walk through in faith and in prayer." That vision has stayed with me to this day. Four years later, our family was doing so many concerts along with the regular church services that we needed a "custom recording" for radio stations and for sale. I figured out that for the price it would cost us to have a studio produce our demo recording ($5,500 at the time), I could purchase one of the little eight-track Fostex recorders that had just come out and produce the album myself! In retrospect, it was a pretty risky venture, but it worked. My Dad agreed to take the risk and I set up a recording studio in my bedroom with my piano, an early version of the drum machine, and a new multitrack cassette recorder. That is how I began to make records.

I was able to produce a recording for the family, and word soon got out about the low cost alternative for custom records. Before long I was busy making records for other people, and I played many of the instruments needed for those recordings. I had never been in a studio, but I was following through with the vision I had received at the age of 14 when I saw equipment that didn't even exist at the time and couldn't play a note on any instrument besides the drums.

It was after I received this vision that I started playing the piano. I just knew that I had to learn to play more instruments in order to fulfill the destiny on my life. I didn't know it then, but I would stay at my parents' little church for 13 more years while God moved and shifted people and circumstances to catapult me from little Red Bay, Alabama, into an international ministry that is reaching around the globe.

My word to you at this point is this: No matter where you live or how forgotten you may feel right now, God knows where you are. He hasn't forgotten you. If you feel that you have a call on your life to preach the gospel, sing before thousands, teach a Sunday school class, or raise godly children, I encourage you to have faith in God. God has not forgotten you and He never will. I had serious doubts about my worth as a person, and I had no musical training to match the prophecies and prayers that people had spoken over me, or to fulfill the grand vision that God planted in my life—but God brought it to pass. Take a stand on this incredible promise from God's unchanging Word:

> *Trust in the Lord with all thine heart; and lean not unto thine own understanding. In all thy ways acknowledge Him, and He shall direct thy paths* (Proverbs 3:5-6).

God knew where Moses was on the back side of the desert and He brought him out in the fullness of time to deliver Israel from Egyptian captivity. He knew where David was in the sheep pasture, and He brought him out as a secret weapon to deliver Israel and become her king. He even remembered an overweight, self-conscious kid who had big dreams in little Red Bay, Alabama. God did it for me and I'll guarantee that He will do it for you!

Chapter 3

A Change Is Coming

*When God decides to use you, He doesn't care
where you're from; and He is capable of taking
you from wherever you are to where He wants
you to be—no matter how impossible it looks.*

The story of David the shepherd has always been
special to me, perhaps because we seem to have so
much in common. We both experienced the frustra-
tion and difficulties of growing up in unknown towns
or rural areas where there were very few people and
even fewer opportunities for those who dreamed of
traveling beyond the boundaries of home. We both
knew that there was a call on our lives, but we had very
little evidence to reassure us that the call was coming
to pass. The good part is that both of us also experienced the faithfulness of God. We learned that He is
well able to transform young shepherds in forgotten
fields into seasoned shepherds and plant them in the
center of His purposes—whether it is a royal palace or
a fiery revival in northern Florida.

I spent almost 18 years in Red Bay, Alabama. I didn't realize it then, but though small towns in the country don't seem to have many opportunities for dreamers, they are often God's chosen proving grounds for His leaders. There are fewer distractions there to drown out the still small voice of God that is so essential to the development of character and vision. (I would learn later in the showbiz environment of Nashville that God can also speak in the midst of chaos and distraction.)

I grew up spending more time around adults than I did with children my own age, so I tended to act and think accordingly. There were always preachers coming to our house after church services, and I would listen by the hour while they talked about their experiences in the ministry and in different places around the world. I suppose I had an inquiring mind, because I always wanted to know more. I wanted to reach beyond my circle of existence to know and experience other things.

I was never comfortable inside the invisible perimeter that so many people wanted to place around me. I have to confess that I was always stepping out of the perimeter or reaching higher than others thought I should have. If anyone in my extended family said that we couldn't do it, then I was determined to figure out a way to reach it. In retrospect, I know it wasn't rebellion driving me—it was curiosity. I was intrigued by what I wasn't supposed to be able to achieve. I have a wonderful extended family composed of good-hearted salt-of-the-earth type of folks, and there are some very talented people among them. But most of them chose to remain close to home and continue doing whatever they have always done. God bless them, and I thank God for them, but I just had to do *something* more than that with my life.

Despite my insecurities about my weight problem and a low self-image, I had a motivation to know and do *more*. Every time I picked up a magazine about Europe, I would dream of going there. I dreamed of seeing the world and of doing things that nobody else would do. I would fantasize about the silliest things because my world was so small—3,000 people and three red lights. As a boy I had traveled all over the country—I was in 46 or 47 states by the time I was eight. I had been around and it was in my blood, so I wasn't happy living in a one-horse town.

Like most preacher's kids, I began to help my father and mother in the work of the ministry as I got older. My musical abilities grew on the organ, piano, bass guitar, and drums, and I began to lead worship at our church after a time. I gradually worked my way into the associate pastor position by trying to help Dad get everything done that needed to get done in a growing church with limited resources. I didn't know it, but God was about to open a great door in my life. Though it bore every sign of failure on the surface, it was literally a key turning point in my life.

Confirmation From Rusty Goodman

From the earliest days of my childhood I had sung songs written by a man named Rusty Goodman and recorded by "The Happy Goodmans." It is probably safe to say that nearly everyone who grew up in Pentecostal or even Evangelical churches in the 1960's, 70's, and 80's, could say the same thing. I can't tell you how many times we sang, "I Wouldn't Take Nothing For My Journey Now" or "Who Am I?" with the unforgettable chorus line, "Who am I that a King would bleed and die for?"

I grew up in a home where we listened to records constantly. My mother even cleaned house to the sounds of the phonograph, and we had a very interesting and diverse set of records. We had all of A.A. Allen's revival records, which came out in all the different colors of vinyl. He was one of the first evangelists on the radio to make live recordings of his services and make them available to listeners. They were "Black Gospel" all the way. Mahalia Jackson was also a popular lady at my house. These records were side by side with records by the Rambos and the Goodman family. I can still sing every Goodman family tune by heart because my parents had every vinyl album the Goodmans ever produced. I knew Rusty Goodman's music as well as I knew the way back home.

By the time I was 17, I had been playing piano for three years, and I went up to audition for Rusty Goodman as a piano player in 1981 or 82. I looked up to

Rusty and I trusted his judgment when it came to gospel music. He told me something that both thrilled me and broke my heart. After I played for him, Rusty said, "Lindell, I love the feel that you have, and I love the way you play. You've got what it takes to do it, but I can't hire you because number one, you can't play in flats, number two you can't play in B [Rusty's favorite key], and you don't know the 'number system.' " He was right; I only played "by ear" and I had never learned how to play in flats. And I didn't know anything about the "Nashville number system." The audition ended with a promise from Rusty. "Lindell, if you'll learn the number system, and if you'll learn how to play in flats, then I want to talk to you. I'll call you in a few years."

I saw myself as a failure in those days, despite the prophecies spoken over me and the destiny I sensed deep in my heart. I think David saw himself that way too. How else could he feel when a great prophet came around to anoint a new king over Israel and his father didn't even bother to include him in the lineup? (See First Samuel 16:10-11.) Later on, despite the prophecies over his life, David must have felt like a dejected failure when he was hiding from King Saul in the cave Adullam (see 1 Sam. 22:1). I saw myself as a fat little preacher's kid living in a backwater town with three traffic lights and no cars, but God sent Rusty Goodman into my life with words of confirmation and what became a prophecy of the future. He was the first professional musician who saw potential in me and said something about it.

If your heart is burning right now, then I'm pretty sure that you need some encouragement too. Don't despair; God never forgets His chosen and obedient servants. God has planted a dream and a set of gifts and abilities in your life, and He is not about to abandon you. Yes, you will almost certainly spend some time in a cave, or in Bethlehem, or in a three-stoplight town on the back side of nowhere, but that doesn't mean you have been forgotten or cast aside.

Becoming a Good Piano Player

I went straight home from that audition with Rusty Goodman and hunted up a friend who showed me how to read number charts according to the Nashville number system. I didn't know it but I was about to meet another God-sent mentor named Lenny LeBlanc.

One night our family ministered at a church pastored by our friend, Henry Melton. It was in this little church that a singer and songwriter named Lenny Le-Blanc first heard me play. Again, you have to understand that I was raised Pentecostal—which meant I was part of a very small, mostly outcast group of Christians who believed in the fullness of the Spirit when it wasn't even remotely popular to do so. On top of that, I was overweight and I never felt attractive. I never felt like anything I did was especially good. I didn't dream that I was even close to being a good musician, but there was something in me that wanted to express my feelings and faith.

Lenny LeBlanc heard me play with my family that night and we struck up a friendship that has lasted to this day. I was working as the youth pastor at Dad's church then, and I invited Lenny to come down to Red Bay in 1983 and do a special service for us. I made up a handbill to advertise and promote the concert and invited every breathing thing on two legs to come.

When Lenny came down he said, "Hey Lindell, I heard you play with your family up at Brother Melton's church. Would you mind learning a few of my songs so you can play with me in the service tonight?" I thought, *Man, I can't play for him! He's from a totally different background and side of the sticks than I am.*

I knew he'd worked extensively around Muscle Shoals, Alabama, which was only 45 miles away. There is an internationally known recording studio there that was renowned for its trademark "groove music" or strong "R&B" (rhythm and blues) influence at the time. Well, I had a strong soulful side in me because I grew up with all those A.A. Allen records, and other albums by Andraé Crouch, Aretha Franklin, and Billy Preston, who had a big hit tune with the line, "Will it go 'round in circles?" I loved that kind of syncopated, high-energy soul style. I loved all the Motown stuff, so I had a good handle on secular music too, but it was different from Lenny's music.

I knew about Lenny's music from his secular days. He had a hit in 1977 or 1978 with a secular group called LeBlanc and Carr. Lenny LeBlanc and Pete Carr recorded a tune called "Falling" that made the Top Ten around the nation. It is still a top tune on all the play lists for most radio stations featuring the "Easy Listening" formats.

When I heard in 1982 that Lenny had been saved and had released a Christian record called "Say A Prayer," I went out and bought it at a record shop. When I listened to it, I thought, *That's a very unusual, clear voice,* and then I realized it was the same guy who sang the secular best-seller, "Falling." I loved the record so much that I wore it out.

So when Lenny LeBlanc told me that he thought I was a good piano player, it really astounded me. Lenny had played with some really great musicians and here I was just a kid. He said, "Lindell, your touch is incredible," and that just built me up. I had no self-confidence whatsoever and I beat myself up with self-doubt and insecurity constantly in those days, but Lenny always believed in me. In the end I agreed to play piano with him that night at my dad's church, and although I wasn't impressed with my playing, evidently he was. After that night, Lenny started asking me to do some of the smaller gigs with him.

This went on for awhile and then Lenny worked with Michelle Pillar on a unique album project at the Muscle Shoals studio with a title song entitled, "Walk Across Heaven With Me." It had a rich "R&B Muscle Shoals" sound that really hit a responsive chord in a time when nearly everyone else in the growing Christian music industry was doing something else. Lenny helped write some of the tunes for the album and worked with Michelle on the production, and when she went on tour, Lenny went along as the front man and performed tunes from his "Say A Prayer" album before she came on. During this time he'd call me and we would do "van gigs" together (short concert engagements within driving distance). We did some things in Houston and Shreveport, and other places in the region. That is how I ended up traveling with Lenny, and that is also how a "prophecy" came to pass.

On a Saturday night in 1984 at the age of 21, I found myself in Shreveport, Louisiana, once again, playing keyboards with Lenny for a Teen Challenge fund-raiser. To my surprise and delight, Rusty Goodman and his accompanist were also playing for the event. I knew he remembered me from the audition three or four years earlier because he came up to me and said, "You were that kid who couldn't play in B flat!"

Then Rusty said, "Lindell, my piano player has gotta go home. He's had an emergency come up. Could you fill in for him since you know all my stuff? You grew up on my music. Would you go ahead and fill in for him tomorrow and tomorrow night? I'll fly you home on Monday."

I had never played for Rusty Goodman since that shaky audition years earlier, but the next day, on Sunday morning, I sat down at a piano and played for him. *Everything he sang was in the key of B.* That was my "crash and burn" test with Rusty. I thank God that I had learned how to play in B! I had never flown in an airplane either. That Monday, Rusty sent me to the airport and told me how to get to the counter and what to do—it was fun. From then on he asked me to play piano for him about once a month or so, and twice a month sometimes. I did some work on Rusty's demos in Nashville recording studios too, and continued to travel with Lenny LeBlanc. The rest of the time I worked in my dad's church on a full-time basis until I was about 27.

I kept busy pursuing my passion from a little-bitty no-name town called Red Bay, Alabama, and God honored it. If nothing else is gleaned from this chapter of my life, I want you to understand this powerful truth: *When God decides to use you, He doesn't care where you're from, and He is capable of taking you from wherever you are, to where He wants you to be, no matter how impossible it looks.*

I know that God used Lenny LeBlanc and Rusty Goodman to train and prepare me for what I am doing today. Even though I moved from a major city to a little town with three stoplights, and even though I had been playing piano for only seven or eight years, God opened the doors for me to travel all over the country with two seasoned Christian artists as a piano player. The traffic lights were the only "high-tech" items in Red Bay, but God had me playing piano in great coliseums, learning about studio work in Nashville, and working with incredibly talented people from every walk of life along the way. I didn't know what I was doing, but God did.

God's Mentors in Action

There are a select few people whom I have been able to connect with on a heart-to-heart level. I'm talking about the kind of relationship that allows you to let your guard down and be yourself all the time in any situation. I've cherished that kind of relationship with Lenny LeBlanc and his wife Sheri since I first met them, and I had that kind of relationship with Rusty and Billie Goodman. I don't know how to define it, but I know we had a shared passion for the most important things in life. I feel like these individuals are family, and I knew from the beginning that they were going to be lifetime friends.

Even though I was intimidated by Lenny LeBlanc's musical background and professional accomplishments, I have had a deep love for Lenny from the beginning. I even felt a certain protectiveness toward Lenny because I had known and served the Lord for many years while Lenny was a young and somewhat vulnerable new believer when I first met him in 1983. Since then he has grown in depth and great wisdom in the Lord, while I managed to enjoy some degree of success in my work along the way, and we remain close to this day. He and Sheri are true friends whom I can always count on.

I enjoyed a different kind of relationship with Rusty Goodman because he was a different kind of man. He was always kind to me, and he was a very good friend and mentor, but I was just a young man in my early 20's while he was a seasoned musician entering his winter years. During the many hours we spent together on difficult road trips and concert tours, Rusty often shared some of the hidden things in his heart. Although Rusty's life was marked by touches of God, which was evident in his music, there was a restlessness beneath the surface. I believe that the heart of the problem stemmed from something he once told me during one of our heart-to-heart talks. He told me that God had called him to preach and he had never heeded that call totally. He chose to stay in the comfort of his music instead, and I think there was a part of him that always regretted it.

I can still remember the time Rusty and I were flying home from a concert appearance somewhere. With a deep sense of longing and even regret in his voice, Rusty turned and confided to me, "You know, Lindell, if I had to do it all over again, I'd have probably been a preacher."

Rusty loved God, and he was very sincere about the Lord, but anyone who knew him—and Rusty himself—would admit that he was as "salty" as the day is long. He came by it honestly. His father was what we call in the South, "a character." He was a Civil War veteran who at the age of 50 married a 25-year-old woman. They had eight children. Anybody who knew Rusty would understand what I'm saying when I say that Rusty Goodman was a very colorful person. He was whimsical and funny, and he was without a doubt one of the most talented men I've ever known. He and Lenny LeBlanc, along with a man named Joey Holder, were the first people in the music business who actually made me believe in myself and the gifts that God had placed in me. They saw potential in me long before I could see it or acknowledge it.

It is important to tell you about Rusty Goodman's music and songwriting ability because they have exerted a strong influence on me today. He was a true mentor to me. Many people think of Rusty Goodman as a strictly "country gospel" man, but the truth is that Rusty had the ability to do virtually anything he wanted to do. Rusty could do pop ballads really, really well. I remember that on one record project he decided to delve into something that he always wanted to do. If you ever pull out his album titled "Family Band," you might be surprised to discover that he slipped in two big band tunes. Rusty had quite a history in music. He was a bass singer, and he used to sing with the Plainsmen. Even people who never listen to country or gospel music have probably heard the tune Rusty sang with the Plainsmen on John Horton's records. If you listen closely to the classic song, "North to Alaska," you will hear Rusty Goodman singing bass.

Rusty's greatest gift as a musician was his ability to reach into the soul of his listeners. He wrote songs with such emotional authority and authenticity that almost any of them could transcend music styles, eras, and even musical tastes. I don't really care for all Southern

Gospel, but I loved Rusty's music and he was considered by many to be one of the fathers of the Southern Gospel world. Personally, I never considered Rusty to be Southern Gospel. He was much larger than any genre because he knew how to touch the soul. As I look back at Rusty's long career as a songwriter, singer, and musician, it is obvious that God squeezed the "call" out of Rusty anyway. He ministered to millions through his music, and his ministry continues to this day through his recordings and timeless songs.

Rusty Goodman's songs still bring tears to my eyes when I hear them. I can name hundreds of them, and in many cases tell you how and why Rusty wrote them. He could write songs that people would sing even when he did it "accidentally." One time he was expressing his irritation with "formula" songwriters who were flooding the market with songs that had no anointing. He told his friends, "I could write a formula song that every Southern Gospel group will sing, and it will be on the charts a year from now." To illustrate his point he selected a verse from Scripture and wrote a formula song called "John the Revelator." Wouldn't you know it—the song went to the top of the charts. In retrospect, the song had Rusty's trademark anointing because he drew from Scripture to write it. The Word of God says, "So shall My word be that goeth forth out of My mouth: it shall not return unto Me void, but it shall accomplish that which I please, and it shall prosper in the thing whereto I sent it" (Is. 55:11).

Rusty was complex, but I believe Rusty genuinely loved the Lord. To even mention Rusty Goodman in my book and name him as a friend is a great honor to me. Although he felt like he hadn't fully answered God's call to the ministry, it is ironic that it was from that point of unsurrendered territory that he wrote his best songs. Rusty and his wife Billie just kind of adopted me back then, and to this day they're special to my heart. Billie is a saint and a prayer warrior who knows how to ring the bells of Heaven.

When Rusty died, it was a big loss for me. I felt like I had lost a father because he believed in me so strongly, and because he was from my past. He connected directly to the very root of my being since I grew up feeding on the anointing in his songs. As I said earlier, Rusty and Lenny were the first two people outside of my family who really believed in my abilities—back when even I didn't believe in them.

I don't really have a great deal of confidence in myself to this day. I don't think I'm particularly a great keyboard player, and I've never considered myself a singer. I think my overactive sinuses make me sound like a nasal head most of the time, but Lenny LeBlanc listened to one of the worship albums from the Brownsville Revival and said, "Man, you sound like Leon Russell leading worship!" That was a compliment to me. Since then I have come to accept the fact that I'm rough and edgy and "black" in my music, even though I'm a white boy. I'm not a black man, but I'm blue-eyed soul.

Passing on the Gift

Any time something valuable is given to one generation, it is expected that the gift, service, or deposit of wisdom will be passed on again to the generations that follow. While I was working in my father's church, someone told me about a young man named Tony Hooper who was about 16 or 17 years old. Tony had been raised in a very strict Pentecostal denomination and had fallen away from the Lord. By the time I met him, he was playing guitar in night clubs with a rock band. Everybody kept saying, "This kid is great! He's a great player—you need to hear him."

I was finally convinced to sit and listen to him play, and the kid was awesome. After we did some music together, I said, "Tony, come play a solo for me at church on Sunday." He said, "Well, I'm not really right with the Lord, so I can't really do that." I told him, "I tell you what. If you come on, then I'll stand responsible before the Lord. Whether you're right or not, just come play the offertory." If I remember correctly, I asked him to play "Amazing Grace" in that service, and when we did it, the Holy Spirit came upon me.

To make a long story short, I recognized that Tony had the hand of the Lord on him. I also knew that Tony knew about the glory of God too, despite his backslidden condition. I don't know to what depth he had explored that, but I knew that he knew about it. I want to mentor people, but I only want to mentor those who know something about the glory and anointing of the Lord. There are a lot of kids who want to plan, who want to do and be something, but it's hard to find those whom the Lord has chosen.

Once you've had a Rusty Goodman or a Lenny Le-Blanc pick you out of a crowd when you didn't feel like you should have been, you are obligated to do the same—generation after generation. That is why I am looking for my "Jonathans" in this present revival at Brownsville. I believe that if we can put them on the front line here right in the middle of revival, then they in turn will be able to take the fire of God to their own generation and those to come.

Something's Coming

Just before my twenty-eighth birthday, I was driving with my dad to a hospital in Florence, Alabama, in the Muscle Shoals area, to do some visitation. I was feeling pretty rough or edgy about something in my spirit, and I said, "Dad, I feel change coming."

He said, "Really?"

"Yeah, and it's going to be major and I'm probably going to leave here."

"Well, why do you believe that?" he asked. (At this time I was his associate pastor.) "I hate to see you leave."

I said, "Well, Dad, I feel like it's destiny. It needs to happen."

He answered, "Where are you going to go?"

"I don't know."

When I was 18 years old, I unconsciously began my preparation for separation from my parents before moving into my adult years. I told my father one day, *"Dad, I want to stop believing everything I believe unless I can find it in the Bible."* For the next year or so, I examined everything I had ever been taught or believed about God and His creation. I discovered that some of the traditional Pentecostal doctrines preached from pulpits everywhere just weren't substantiated in the Bible. On the other hand, there were times when certain things happened in the Bible, but they were never trumpeted as doctrines of the Church.

Week after week and month after month, I corralled my father with my probing questions and we dialogued about the Word of God until we found peace. In the end, my father stopped preaching certain things when he confirmed that they were man's tradition instead of God's Word. I didn't set out to upset my father or challenge authority just to be rebellious, and my father knew it. In the end, my respectful search for truth helped both of us walk closer to the truth and closer together, and it prepared me to be a leader. I can tell you today that I'm not a person who accepts just anything because everybody thinks it's good. Show it to me in the Word, friend.

I didn't realize that God was helping me to establish the basics in my heart and mind so I could go on to even tougher areas of discernment and judgment. I was about to enter one of the most confusing and frustrating times of my life, a time when I wondered if I had heard God correctly or even if I had heard Him at all.

When I look back at my life today, I thank God for every teacher and guide He sent my way in those early days, and at the top of my list are my own father and mother, then Rusty and Billie Goodman, and Lenny LeBlanc.

Chapter 4

Nashville's Most Reluctant Immigrant Arrives

In the two months after I told Dad that I felt a big change was coming, I had three offers from churches seeking worship leaders. One call came from Pastor Johnny Wade Sloan at Hamilton Christian Center, an aggressive church of about 800 people in Hamilton, Ohio, just outside of Cincinnati. The second offer came from Harvest Time Tabernacle, a rapidly growing church pastored by Kemp C. Holden, Jr., in Arkansas. I'd met Pastor Holden prior to that time, and he remembered me when he began searching for a minister of worship. The third call came from an obscure little church in Norwalk, California, which is a Los Angeles County suburb just outside of Los Angeles. It was only a few freeway exits away from Buena

Park and Disneyland in Anaheim (although that knowledge did *not* influence my final decision).

I already knew Don Metcalf, the pastor of the church in Norwalk, because I had preached and performed in concert there the year before. This church had around 150 people in attendance, and Brother Don was a real go-getter, as well as a very kind person. When I started praying, I told my dad that I was going to go to one of these three places. Finally Don called back and said, "Look, Lindell, here's the offer."

I told him, "I tell you what, Don, here's what I'll do. I'll come out there, but let's agree that at the end of six months, if I'm not happy with it or if you're not happy with it, then we'll go our separate ways and remain friends. Truthfully, Don, I haven't heard the voice of the Lord on this. I just know I'm supposed to leave Red Bay, and I can't get clear direction on which of the three offers I should take. I'm just going to go for the most adventurous instead of the steady ones. You're trying to build a church there, so let's do it."

When I told Dad my decision, he said, "Lindell, just take a couple keyboards, your clothes, and your car, and go." Instead of listening to the wisdom of my father about taking just a few things with me, I loaded up my entire bedroom recording studio (which by this time had grown to a massive scale), crammed everything into a U-Haul, and drove to California.

In the months before I left Red Bay, I spent a lot of time with Tony Hooper, establishing him in the faith and training him to lead worship. When I finally left my home church in January of 1991, I officially turned over my duties as worship leader to Tony. Leaving home was the most painful thing I'd ever done because I was leaving behind virtually every earthly anchor and support system in my life. I left my home church, my family, my mom and dad, and my familiar ministry functions in Dad's church to move all the way to Los Angeles, some 3,000 miles away. I guess Don sensed that it might be a difficult trip for me, so he flew to Alabama and met me in the grand metropolis of Red Bay to make the long trek with me to California.

I knew I had to leave because it was the only way to break the strong bond I had with my mother and father so I could go on to fulfill my destiny. I think they knew it too. I had entered the season of transition when I had to launch out on my own. My parents were *never* controlling or overbearing, and I was by no means overdependent on them. The truth is that everyone reaches a point in life when he or she needs to establish a totally separate identity outside of his or her parents' home. That doesn't mean the need for parental advice, support, and even assistance is over, but it does mean that a permanent change and transfer of ultimate responsibility has come. Any parental assistance after this point of independence is normally temporary in nature. I was about to accept personal responsibility for my own life and destiny. We cried and reminisced and hugged and shot the inevitable "good-bye photos" and then it was time.

I got in the U-Haul truck with Don and we waved as we pulled away from the place I'd called home for almost 18 years. We had already entered the endless state of Texas when the Gulf War broke out, and Don and I listened to the almost continuous radio reports of the battles into the night hours as we followed the sun's course westward. I ended up living in Don's house for four months, and we had many a long talk together about the things of God. Don is a very wise man and he's a good man. It became clear that God had placed yet another godly mentor in my path to make a deposit in me. I grew to love Don and his family during my stay there, and it was a good experience all the way around—except that I knew at the end of six months that I wasn't supposed to be there. I was in L.A. from January through October of '91, and at the end of the six-month period we had agreed upon, I said, "Don, I can't stay."

He said, "What are you going to do?"

"Well, I don't know," I replied. When I decided to go to Los Angeles to help Don, there were three doors open to me. Now there were none. I called my parents and said, "Look, I don't know what to do. I know I'm not supposed to be here in California, but there are no doors open. What should I do?"

Of course my dad said, "Well, come on home." I answered, "Well, there's nothing to do there, Dad. I've already replaced myself there." He said, "We'll think of something, son." It didn't take much convincing. I said in mock reluctance, "Well, okay." (It was time for some "temporary" parental assistance again.)

I loaded everything back up into a semi-tractor trailer (somehow everything seemed to expand in the California sun), and that in itself was a character-building experience. Each time I picked up yet another piece of recording equipment, I shook my head and thought to myself, "Boy, Dad was right. Yes sir, Dad was right. Dad was right. I should have packed light."

Hurry Up and Wait

When I analyzed the California situation, I knew there weren't any problems between Don and I, and there never were. California just wasn't where I was supposed to be, and I knew it. I had already worked my way through the months of pain involved in breaking off from my family, and I had developed a new base of friends in California. I was producing some custom records in L.A. and having a blast, but I still knew that I wasn't supposed to be there. But why should I go back to Red Bay? It was home. If I was going to have to struggle across a spiritual desert to fulfill my calling, then I might as well do my struggling back home.

Once again I felt the thrill of waiting for Red Bay's three infamous traffic lights to change from red to green the day I drove into town in early October of 1991. Perhaps I should have seen the pattern of "hurry up and wait" at the nearly deserted intersections with stoplights as a sign of what awaited me in the spirit realm, but to me it was just another day in Red Bay. My parents love me dearly and I love them just as much, but

I told them I would not lead worship or do anything musically at the church but play piano. I didn't want to cast a shadow over what Tony was doing. The last thing I wanted to do was to march back into the church sanctuary and say, "Well, I'm back, and I'm the preacher's kid. I want my job back, so you're out."

I somehow managed to sit in a pew when I returned, but I also managed to help Dad in other ways. He didn't really have an office set up at the church building, so I established an office for him and I regularly went in and did clerical work (another character-building exercise for me—I hate office work). I just wanted to help Dad get off the ground in that area.

October, November, and December of 1991 were the most miserable months I can remember in my life. Every day and every night were consumed with constant questions that challenged my worth and reason for existence. "What am I doing here? Where am I going? What am I going to do? This is stupid, what is this about?" I was 28 years old, and over and over again the nagging thought plagued my mind, "Oh my God, I messed up. There is nobody who wants me now. Here I am at a place where I don't even want to be." I was miserable with a capital "M."

Early in December and late in my agonizing season of searching and questioning, I was helping Mom and a close friend put up a Christmas tree when the phone rang. It was Michael Sykes, the man who married Rusty and Billie Goodman's daughter, Tanya. Michael said, "Lindell, I just had lunch with Landy and Joy Gardner, and they are looking for an assistant." Michael and Tanya were good friends and they really believed in me, even though I was having serious doubts at that time. Landy Gardner was the choir director in charge of all music at Christ Church, one of the largest churches in Nashville, Tennessee. Michael had told me earlier that Landy used to go through peaks and valleys when he wanted to quit working with the choir. He'd tell Michael and Tanya, "I can't do this. I'm not even a musician. I don't need to be directing this choir." The truth is that he was an anointed choir director, but at that time he also had to function as worship division leader and music team leader.

Michael had something else to tell me this time. "And Lindell, he wants you to come up and train for it. He said he's interested in you. I asked him some questions about why he wants to quit and what he needs, and I told him you could do everything they need."

I said, "Well, you lied, Mike."

He said, "No, *you can do anything you need to.*"

"Well, thank you, Mike."

Michael wasn't about to be put off. He said, "Now here's Landy's number. You need to call him." I jotted down the number but I was determined not to make the call. My parents were curious about the phone call, but I tried to turn every conversation toward our Christmas tradition of mad shopping in Atlanta.

For years we had set aside a week in December for this tradition. Since we lived in a small town, we would always get in our car early in the morning on the first or second Monday in December and drive to Atlanta, Georgia, or Birmingham, Alabama, to do our Christmas shopping in a bigger city. This year we headed to Atlanta and booked a motel for three days. Then we shopped till we dropped, just me and my mom and dad, with occasional breaks to eat out at good restaurants. I won't lie to you—it was fun.

It Pays to Listen to Parents

My parents knew I had Landy's number with me in Atlanta, but I told them I wasn't going to call him because, "All they want at that church is somebody to push papers. Landy's the director, see. All they want is somebody to push papers, and I am not going to do that job. I know how big churches work, and I don't want the job."

Things finally came to a head on Tuesday night in Atlanta. I'd gone through a whole year of turmoil with my stay in L.A. and my trip back home, topped with three solid months of misery. I was laying in bed and we were about to go to sleep when my father said, "Son, are you going to call Landy?"

"No, I don't think so," I said. "It's just another one of those dumb offers." The truth was that I really didn't know how big Christ Church was, and I knew nothing about the size of its staff or its ministry style. All I knew was that Tanya Goodman Sykes enjoyed singing in the choir that Landy Gardner directed, and that they had recorded some tapes. Despite my ignorance, I told

Dad, "It just sounds like a church that's wanting a 'hey you' gopher."

I was a little surprised by Dad's question because my parents weren't the interfering type. If they pressed a point, there was usually a pretty strong motivation behind it (and I was pretty sure what their motivation was this time). "Well, why do you want me to call?" I asked them as I stared at the dark ceiling of the hotel room.

This was my mother's cue. She said, "Because you're miserable, and you know you shouldn't allow an opportunity that comes to you to go by—especially when you're miserable—without at least calling to see what they want."

"I know what they want. They want…" and then I just rehearsed my standard line about a "hey you" again. I was just blabbing and my mother knew it.

"You don't know that; you haven't talked to them," Mom said. "We just want to see you happy, and you're driving us crazy because you're so miserable."

The next morning I got up and called Landy (I was learning that it pays to listen to parents—even when you are an adult). Landy was so cordial and kind on the phone that he totally disarmed me. His great spirit of hospitality just melts your heart. He said, "Lindell, I'm not qualified for this job. I want somebody to come in here and be trained to fill my position so that in a couple of years I can let them have it."

I thought to myself, "Well, he sounds pretty serious to me." Then Landy asked me what I could do, and after we covered some basics, we agreed that I would need to go to Nashville to try out for the position. Landy said he would call me with the details but I didn't hear from him until February. For awhile I thought he really wasn't interested, but then he called and said, "Can you come up in the middle of February?"

From Red Bay to...Nashville?

I'll never forget the day I arrived in Nashville and drove up to Christ Church. I was Nashville's most reluctant immigrant that day, and something in me was so overwhelmed at the massive size of the church building that for a moment I almost missed those three lonely stoplights in Red Bay, Alabama. I interviewed for the job, and every time I'd talk about my convictions or preferences in certain areas of music or worship, Landy would nod and say, "Yeah, yeah, oh yeah." I was beginning to feel some excitement stir in my heart again, but I wasn't sure of the thing until I heard Associate Pastor Dan Scott preach at Christ Church that Sunday night. It was just like this guy was talking directly to me about my destiny and what I needed to do.

At that point I said silently to myself, *Okay.* So I got in Landy's car and we drove out to a restaurant where I told him, "Landy, I'll take the job, but you need to know something."

"What?"

"I can't really read music well, but I know some basic theory." I said, "I'll tell you what, Landy. If you give me the job, then in a year I'll be able to write any chart you want." He smiled and said, "No problem."

I took the job and I was immediately overwhelmed. I had just moved from a church that measured 40 by 80 feet (which seemed big to me in those days) to a 3,000-seat church in Nashville that looks like a big shopping center towering from a perch on a hill. From the first day I walked in there I was thinking, *Now these people seem to admire me, but can I do what they want me to do? I've never worked on something of this scale—this is the "big time."*

Christ Church was pastored by L.H. Hardwick, a man who in every way exemplified a true father of the faith, and a genuine pastor. Landy Gardner was the (basically) volunteer choir director. I was the new (and the first) minister of music. Landy had served as choir director there for 17 years, and he was paid a token salary to direct the choir only. I was hired to pull the service together, lead worship in the services, and find the choir songs (along with Landy and his wife). Once the songs were chosen, Joy Gardner (Landy's wife) and I would arrange them. Then I would rehearse the musicians and take care of everything so that all Landy had to do was direct the choir. I don't want to minimize Landy's role. He had an uncanny ability to understand when something worked or didn't work, and he taught me a great deal in this area even though he wasn't a musician by traditional definition. He was incredibly creative and very "artsy."

Landy was a respected interior designer whose multi-million dollar design company is probably ranked among the top ten design firms in the Eastern United States. He has done things for *Southern Living* magazine and others. The interior design work he has done is palatial. It's incredible. Joy Gardner was a Dove Award recipient and a skilled artist in her own right. She stayed very busy as a background vocalist in Nashville studios, and she had the best "ear" for part arrangements that I have ever known. Joy always sang from the depths of her emotions, and everyone who heard her was touched.

Landy had a tremendous ability to feel the music. He had an intuitive understanding of what it should be. He could tell you if an ending of a song or arrangement would work or not. Now, he couldn't tell you the musical theory to back up his observations; he would just tell you when it wasn't right. Joy and I would work on a song until the parts were right, and then we'd rehearse them. That's when he'd say, "Now this part right here, it needs more lift, it needs more punch. And this part needs to come down a little bit. We need a little key change here." He was like a skilled overseer. Landy Gardner was (and still is) one of God's great "music designers."

I have to confess that I was intimidated by Landy in the beginning, but I connected immediately with Joy, who seemed at times to be the sister I never had. I was basically a country bumpkin moving into the city, and even though I knew a lot, and had a lot of raw talent, I was painfully aware that I had never practiced my craft and calling in the real world. My first opportunity to do this came at one of the largest churches in a city renowned as a music industry Mecca. Famous musicians, songwriters, composers, arrangers, and producers were in attendance at virtually every service.

So when I hired on at Christ Church, I was the *first full-time staff member* the music department had ever employed. I put in about 60 to 80 hours a week if you count my day hours and the endless rehearsals at night. I had no support staff. Even though Christ Church at that time was running about 3,600 each Sunday, the music department had no secretary and not one computer. I had to answer all phone calls myself, and we had a choir of more than 200 people. I was responsible for the production of the services every Sunday, and Sunday night I led worship. I also had a praise team that I had to rehearse, along with the two-hour choir rehearsal on Wednesday nights. Then I also had to rehearse the band. On top of all that, in the beginning I had to be at the office every single day like the rest of the church staff (although they did not keep night hours like I did), and I personally followed up on about 80 to 90 calls a week or more.

That was the normal schedule. Then there were the busy times—like the five or six times a year we toured with the choir. My responsibilities included all the logistics of getting us there and back, and adjusting to all the sound system situations. It was easy to log in 80 or more hours a week trying to keep up with all that. It was a difficult, stretching experience that I wouldn't wish on anybody, but I praise God that when I went through it, I got to work with people like Landy and Joy Gardner, whom I dearly love and respect. Landy always "expected to get what he expected," and he always wanted it right. I worked myself to a frazzle to give it to him too, because I respected him and because it is my nature to be very loyal to my coworkers and leaders. (I wouldn't be in Brownsville today if I hadn't allowed God to develop these qualities in me through hard work and adversity.)

So I basically had a church of thousands and a staff of one. I had to create a department from thin air. (I don't know how Landy and Joy functioned without a support staff for 17 years.) When I left Christ Church later on, the church hired two people plus a secretary to take my place. I was able to accomplish what I did because I was young and single, and I had no social life or distractions outside of my work, except for some personal record producing on the side. (We will explore the church workplace and job expectations in detail in Chapter 10—it is a chapter you won't want to miss if you are a musician, a worship leader, a church administrator, or a pastor.) The only social life I had was with Landy and his wife, but fortunately I did a lot of things with them, and they were a riot.

Motives of the Heart

Landy and Joy weren't my only mentors in Nashville. God imported one from Germany via Texas just to readjust my attitudes about the motivations of my heart. Three weeks after I moved to Nashville, I was walking down a hallway in the massive Christ Church complex when I heard a woman say, "Hey, Lindell." When I looked over I saw a little staunch-looking bleached-blonde German woman about my mother's age. She looked at me and said, "Come here." So I walked into her office and said, "Yes, what can I help you with?" She said, "My name is Joy Wright." Then she stood up and said, "You are here for a different reason than what you think you came for."

"What does that mean?" I asked.

"That means that God sent you here to teach the people of this church something about worship that they don't know." Then she added, "In the process there is going to be some changing going on in you, too." I stood there with my mouth gaping, thinking to myself, *Now this gutsy lady has got to be the most feisty thing I have every seen in my life. She just looked at me and let it rip!* I just had to like someone like Joy Wright.

I learned later that Joy had been the administrative assistant for Church on the Rock International, which was founded by Dr. Larry Lea in 1983 at Rockwall, Texas. When I met her, she had moved to Nashville and was using her administrative skills for L.H. Hardwick and Global Christian Ministries, a national network of pastors. I have always tried to surround myself with people who aren't afraid to correct me when it's necessary. I like the idea of associating with somebody who has guts enough to say, "No, that can't happen, and here is why..." Honest friends and counselors can save you a lot of grief—if you carefully consider what they have to say before acting on a matter.

That first encounter at Christ Church was the beginning of what I believe will be a lifelong friendship with Joy Wright. The Lord definitely put Joy in my life, although it was a unique relationship considering the fact that she was a widow with sons who were my age. She was always blunt with me, and she asked me hard questions that would not go away. These were questions such as, "Have you ever considered your motivations for doing this? Have you every considered why you do what you do?" It was after I met Joy Wright in Nashville that I began to seriously examine my motives for ministry and music on a continuous basis. I was learning firsthand that God is interested in the motives of the heart.

Another important discovery I made in my first few weeks at Christ Church was that God had His hand on Landy Gardner. Now Landy loves God, but he didn't feel like he was the one who should be the choir director at Christ Church. I soon realized that no matter how long I was there, I would never be the man in charge. It wasn't because of Landy; it was because God had ordained it that way. Landy's function and office was an ordained divine thing. Joy Wright was right—I was there for some purpose other than to replace Landy and become choir director of Christ Church.

Once I understood the situation and accepted it in my heart, I realized that one of the reasons I was brought to Nashville was to *learn*. From February 1992 to January 1994, I assisted Landy at Christ Church and God used those two years as "college" to hone my gifts and abilities. I focused my energies and applied myself to learn, learn, learn. I had a promise to keep to Landy, and I kept it. I learned how to write music charts as I'd promised, and much more. Meanwhile, God was again making great changes in my character.

A Real Learning Time

Christ Church was very prominent in Nashville, and Landy had some powerful connections in that city. His highly respected interior design firm served the "Who's Who" of Nashville. Since he had developed such an excellent choir, the Christ Church choir ended up in some of the most unexpected places—like the Country Music Association (CMA) Awards television special, which was broadcast live from Nashville coast to coast.

The Christ Church choir was asked to perform "Put A Little Love In Your Heart" with Dolly Parton for the grand finale of the 1993 CMA Awards. We went in the studio about a week before the show, but the word was that Dolly Parton was having trouble with her voice even then. The producers wanted a special arrangement with the choir that stretched Dolly's hit tune to last a full 16 minutes, and Landy was out there trying to get life out of us for that long. Two days before the CMA Awards Show she lost her voice totally. The CMA people called me at Christ Church and said, "Look, Dolly can't talk. Now you guys helped record the background for 'Put A Little Love in Your Heart' as the finale of the show. We're two days down from the show and Dolly can't talk. We've got to have a finale. Look, can you come up with something in case she can't sing? Is there a hymn or something that's kind of a sing-along-song everybody knows that we can close with?" I said, "I'll think of something."

I started pondering the problem, and I knew things were in bad shape. The night before the show, Dolly came back to the recording studio along with her backup singer, who was a strong Christian and a member of Christ Church. Dolly could barely manage a whisper and her voice was getting worse. Her backup singer asked to be excused and walked around the block, praying, "Lord, should I ask her to let me pray for her? I don't want to be too forceful."

Finally she returned to the studio and quietly asked Dolly, "I know it's really important that you be able to sing for the CMA show. Is it all right with you if I pray for you?"

Dolly nodded and the two went into the ladies' room where the singer laid hands on Dolly Parton and prayed. After prayer, Dolly walked out into the studio, looked up at the producer in the control room, and said in a clear voice, "Roll the tape!" While they all looked on in shock, Dolly sang that high-powered 16-minute vocal arrangement all the way through without a single mistake on the first "take" or recording pass. Then she promptly lost her voice again. So for the finale of the CMA Awards show the following evening, Dolly Parton pantomimed, or lip-synched, through the whole song to the accompaniment of a rejoicing Christ Church choir. No one else may have known, but more than 200 people in the choir and one very talented celebrity knew that millions of people around the world were literally listening to a miracle that night—even though we were all lip-synching.

During my stay at Christ Church, I was also able to work with Landy and the choir in recording projects with Garth Brooks, Reba McEntire, and Michael W. Smith. It was a real learning time for me. (I was very impressed with Michael because he was genuinely humble and down to earth.)

A number of celebrities attended Christ Church, including Naomi and Wynonna Judd. On my first Sunday on the job in 1992, I was a little country nobody from nowhere who didn't particularly listen to country music. Landy was taking me around to all the church introducing me as his new assistant. We finally reached the pastor's office, and Landy took me up to a lady dressed in a long white dress with light boots. Her hair was in a pony tail and she was wearing hardly any makeup. Landy introduced me as the new music director and his assistant, but never mentioned the lady's name. We talked to her for three or four minutes, and were getting ready to leave when I said, "Well, it was a pleasure to meet you. By the way, what is your name?"

"I'm Wynonna Judd."

I stammered something like, "Gosh, you don't look like your pictures."

On the night we were rehearsing for the CMA Awards, Wynonna was scheduled to rehearse her song just before the finale. She was leaving the stage as we were coming on, and I was out there on the stage when Wynonna walked up to me and stared at my face. "Is this your first in the Grand Old Opry?"

"Yes, it is."

"I just wanted to introduce myself. I'm Wynonna Judd."

I said, "I really apologize for that, but honestly, I really didn't know who you were."

Wynonna just laughed and said, "Actually, it was very refreshing. It was nice for somebody not to know who I was."

"Well, I surely didn't mean to offend you, but I just didn't know who you were."

My tenure at Christ Church was an unforgettable time for me, yet all along I knew it was only for a season. Landy and Joy Gardner were responsible for exposing me and the Christ Church choir to some incredible opportunities and learning experiences in music and ministry. They were also mentors to me.

There was one area where I was to be a mentor to them, however.

With each month that passed by, my understanding of God's call upon Landy's life and his reluctance toward that call became clearer and clearer. Finally the time came when I knew my time was up. To this day Landy and Joy Gardner remain my good friends, but I knew I had a prophetic assignment to fulfill involving Landy that wasn't going to be pleasant. God wanted me to be a true friend to Landy. That meant that I had to tell him the truth about certain things in his life and ministry. I knew he didn't really want to hear them, but God had placed me in a position to say them with authority, and I knew that they had to be said before I could leave.

There's a Price to Pay

No matter who you are or what you feel God has ordained you to do, you will never fulfill your destiny or anointing or calling alone. God always mates godly character with His supernatural gifts and callings. My six-month stint in California built character into me. My agonizing three-month wilderness of confused and heartbroken searching built even more character into me. My struggles to expand and stretch myself to fulfill my tasks at Christ Church in Nashville also built character into me. All along the way God sent godly men and women who spoke into my life and brought wisdom, correction, and instruction that built my character and honed my gifts and abilities.

Examine the lives and ministries of the apostles, and particularly of the apostle Paul. God sent prophets like Agabus and Barnabas into Paul's life to help guide and disciple him along his journey through opportunities and trials. Later on, Paul did the same for his young disciples. If there is a call on your life, then you can be sure you will experience tests and trials, and that God will send instructors into your life. These experiences are absolutely necessary to develop the character traits you will need to properly carry and direct your spiritual gifts and natural talents. Every great call of God comes at a price. The rewards are beyond counting, but the trials can sometimes seem more than you can possibly bear. Don't look to the side, and don't look back. Keep your hand on the plow and your eyes on the goal Jesus has set before you (see Lk. 9:62).

And He [Jesus] said to them all, If any man will come after Me, let him deny himself, and take up his cross daily, and follow Me. For whosoever will save his life shall lose it: but whosoever will lose his life for My sake, the same shall save it (Luke 9:23-24).

Chapter 5

Loose From My Roots

In December of 1993, the Lord released me from my assignment to Christ Church. When I dropped a hint about it to Landy by saying, "Well, I ought to just quit sometime," his response was typical. "You're out of your mind! Why would you quit?"

By the time New Year's Day of 1994 rolled around, Landy knew I was planning to leave for certain, and he didn't get where he is as a businessman by being laid back. He did his best to change my mind, but it didn't work. "What are you going to do—flounder around? Do nothing with yourself?" he asked me in exasperation. "You know what, Lindell? You're going to do like all those other musicians—you're going to mess around and miss God. Now you've got a lot of potential here." Then he asked me a perfectly logical question. "Well, do you know where you're going to go or what you are going to do?"

I looked into Landy's eyes and said, "Landy, I have no idea where I'm going. All I know is that my time is up at Christ Church. It has nothing to do with you or the church. You and Joy are my friends and you've treated me right, and the church is great. The truth is that the Lord has told me my time is up here. I don't know what He has for me yet, but I do know it's not here."

I knew Landy well enough to know that it would take him some time to adjust to my decision emotionally. At first he would be upset with me because I was leaving—regardless of my reasons or rationale. I knew it would take him about three or four weeks to adjust to the idea, so I just waited. After the smoke cleared, Landy called me and said, "Lindell, do you want to go to lunch?"

Over lunch at a nearby restaurant, I looked at Landy and said, "You may not receive this from me at this time, but I have something to tell you." He was still listening so I said, "You can call it prophecy, foresight, or whatever you want, but Landy, *the hand of the Lord is upon you to direct the choir at Christ Church.* So what I say is this: Find a young student who can fill in on a part-time basis whom you can train right here in the church. Or, you can look for someone whose ministry calling and preference is to be the second man. He should be someone who has no problem fulfilling the role as your assistant. Landy, there are guys out there who are capable, and who don't want the front line. That would be the perfect solution for you.

I am happy to report that Landy and Joy Gardner and I have maintained our friendship. To be sure, there was a time early in 1994 when we were estranged because of the tension created by my departure from Christ Church. I stayed away long enough for the new man who had taken my place to adjust to his new position without my presence. It was during this time that I spent a lot of time talking with Joy Wright and visiting with a married couple connected with a major ministry in the Nashville area.

Days of Searching

My days after Christ Church were days of searching, probing, and questioning. That is when Joy steered me toward the writings of some of the greatest writers and thinkers of the modern Church. I began to devour books written by Oswald Chambers, Gene Edwards, and A.W. Tozer. She gave me a copy of *The Pursuit of God* by Tozer, and the passion for truth and holiness I saw in this book and others just really set me on fire.

When I stepped down from my position at Christ Church, I also stopped attending services there regularly. Then I did something that horrified Joy Wright—I began attending St. Bartholomew's Episcopal Church in Nashville.

When I told her about St. Bartholomew's (or "St. B's"), Joy said, "Yeah, I know you like it and all, but it'll make you a *cross-kisser*, Lindell!"

I replied, "I'll tell you what, Joy—have you ever been to an Episcopal church?"

"No."

I said, "Get ready. I'll be by to pick you up in 15 minutes—you're going to church with me."

The Lord seems to delight in sending the most unlikely people into our lives to help form the character of Christ in us. God used my phone conversations with Joy Wright and with Landy's wife (also named Joy) to help me maintain balance during my searching phase. Landy's wife has a real Pentecostal heritage, and we often talked about prayer and the revival in Toronto.

Joy Wright not only became my "literary counselor," but she also felt the call to correct my skewed views on marriage. She dismissed all the times I said that I would never marry. To cope with the complications I ran into as a single music minister traveling and working in churches, I had put up a barrier to keep women out of my life. I had decided not to have anything to do with women because, "After all, they are all alike." Joy challenged that kind of narrow thinking and showed me that there were a lot of things I needed to learn. After all, I wasn't her first "patient." She had also guided two of her own sons through the relationship rapids of the young and restless. Even in a strange city far from home, God gave me another family that we affectionately (and creatively) referred to as "the family."

Its members included Joy and I, with Bill and René Morris, and Gary and Toni Oliver. All of us traveled or ministered on weekends, so we would get together during the week to swap stories, share good food, and enjoy one another's fellowship. It was a real stabilizing factor in my life and a source of encouragement. Joy just kept sticking my Pentecostal roots back in my face during a time when I almost left them behind.

I was drawn toward liturgy during that time period because it was something I didn't know existed. Many young people who come from Pentecostal roots will go either to the extreme of walking as closely to the edge of sin as they can without falling headlong, or they will gravitate toward the things their soul longed for but didn't find in Pentecostal circles. I know that I longed to see the majesty and awesome power of God. I longed for stability that wasn't swayed by emotions or circumstances. I wanted to feel the bigness and holiness of God untainted by too much familiarity. I found these things in some measure at St. Bartholomew's. (Today, I can tell you that they are present in true revival too, along with all the tremendous strengths of Pentecost.) In retrospect, I think one of the greatest areas of longing in my life centered around the Lord's supper, or holy communion.

What Happened to Communion?

Somehow, somewhere, the Pentecostal world lost or removed the power, the awe, and the reverence that should always be present around the Lord's table. Perhaps we went too far to one side in trying to oppose some of the extremes perceived in some of the high church practices and teachings, but I am convinced that we went too far. We robbed ourselves of one of the most powerful gifts and privileges in the New Covenant under Christ.

The high church traditions were created as a protection and countermeasure against wrong doctrine and unbiblical emotional movements that pleased the flesh while violating the Word. The Pentecostal movement sprang up in the midst of spiritual coldness and lifelessness, when the organized church had nearly had the life snuffed out of it by clergy who had come to worship the letter of the law more than the Spirit who gave it life. They had begun to rely on rituals (some of which were based on solid scriptural commandments) to save rather than on a personal repentance and a saving relationship with Christ Himself. Something inside me longed for a balance between the righteous fear of God and the gentle intimacy we have through Jesus. I wanted to be reminded of the unsearchable greatness of God, whether it came through the sounds of a majestic pipe organ that shook glass, stone, and beam; or through the solemn silence of reverent prayer in a great cathedral.

More than anything else, I wanted to experience the true power of communion. Somehow the living Christ and the sense of His great sacrifice on Calvary are lost when tasteless, paper-thin wafers are passed along on a converted offering plate down a pew filled with distracted worshipers once a month (if that often). The power in the blood of the Lamb evaporates somewhere between the pouring of the Welch's grape juice and the noisy slurping and hurried "cup stacking" rituals (yes, I said *rituals*) in our churches. I don't expect every Pentecostal, Charismatic, or Spirit-filled church to suddenly turn into Episcopal or Lutheran churches, but I do passionately pray that all of us will rediscover the wonder and life-changing power of communion.

I long to see us all raise our standards a bit and honor the words of Jesus as Holy Writ. *Three times* He specifically told us to do something concerning communion. He gave us two ways to remember Him, and together they show or demonstrate the reality of His death and resurrection until His return. He even gave us a guideline for how often we are to do these things. As a Pentecostal, I have to ask why it appears that we only remember Jesus Christ 4 to 12 times a year in communion? I didn't set the standard—Jesus did. There is something in my heart that shouts with passion, "How dare we trivialize something that was obviously so important to our Master?!"

> *And when He had given thanks, He brake it, and said, Take, eat: this is My body, which is broken for you: **this do in remembrance of Me**. After the same manner also He took the cup, when He had supped, saying, This cup is the new testament in My blood: this do ye, as oft as ye drink it, **in remembrance of Me**. For as often as ye eat this bread, and drink this cup, **ye do show the Lord's death till He come*** (1 Corinthians 11:24-26).

Now that I've preached my sermon on communion, I have to mention the role that my dear friend Dan

Scott played in my life. It was Dan's passionate preaching that convinced me I needed to come to Christ Church in the first place, and it was his passion for the deep things of Christ that led me to look more closely at the Lord's table and the whole new world of liturgy.

Dan was a second-generation missionary when he came to Christ Church. He understood sacrifice because he was raised on the mission field. He worked his way all the way to a Master's degree in his quest for knowledge. He didn't intend to throw out our Pentecostal roots, but he longed to replace our extra-biblical "Pentecostal tomfoolery" with true godly experience.

Dan Scott was against the "false Pentecost" he saw permeating the modern Church, but he was very much for the true Pentecostal experience born out of an intimate encounter with God. He also saw a rich vein of genuine godliness in the liturgy that was so misunderstood by many. He believed that this would only enrich our Pentecostal walk by giving it a foundation that went further back than Azusa Street (and he would never belittle that important rebirth of fire in the Church).

I need to emphasize that whatever our views may be about communion, liturgy, ritual, or miracles, Jesus didn't give us any slack in how we are to treat one another. He said, "By this shall all men know that ye are My disciples, if ye have love one to another" (Jn. 13:35). We can disagree, but we must love one another.

Missing the Glory

During my worst moments, at the times when I was closest to going over the edge of casting away my Pentecostal heritage, I walked around with a continual heaviness on me. Most people would laugh if I went into the details of what bothered me (because they would seem so insignificant to most people), but I have to tell you that once you have tasted the glory of the Lord and sensed His overwhelming presence, it doesn't take much disobedience or separation from the holy to grieve your spirit. During my search for "something" outside of my Pentecostal experience, I was associated professionally with a few people who didn't live what we would call a holy life. It wore on me because even though I didn't sin in the way most people think of sinning, I still sensed a certain grieving going on inside.

I believe that everyone who experiences the glory of God has taken an unspoken "Nazarite vow of the Holy Ghost," whether they know it or not. There is an internal rule of righteousness put in our hearts that we just don't want to cross for fear of losing that precious glory. We can't bear the thought of forfeiting the abiding presence of God that we have tasted. That is why Joy's constant insistence that I not waver from my Pentecostal roots was so vital to my spiritual health—it became an important anchor during my most difficult times in Nashville. She constantly reminded me, "This [the music business] is not what you're here for. It's not what you're called for. It's not your final destiny. God has something better for you."

I was really soaking in the reverence for God that I saw at St. Bartholomew's Episcopal Church, and I was feeding on the fire that I saw in the writings of Tozer and Oswald, as well as on the steadfast faith that I saw in C.S. Lewis' writings. Yet there was also something in me that grieved over my disenchantment with my Pentecostal roots.

Part of the problem was that my roots were good roots. Although I had seen a lot of abuses in my years growing up in the Pentecostal church and traveling in the ministry with my parents, I had also seen how things *should be done.* My parents went out of their way to instruct and warn me about the pitfalls that can destroy a ministry or a personal testimony. They taught me the importance of integrity. They had worked with tent preachers and traveling ministries for decades, and they had seen a lot of abuses.

One time they were working for a tent preacher who had received a very large offering during an evening service attended by several thousand people who started giving their jewelry and watches in the offering (like Rolexes and diamond rings). When the evangelist went back to the motel, he called in my parents. Mom said, "We walked in the room, and when we looked at their king-size bed, they had the money and the offerings spread out and they were counting it." She said the evangelist's wife was lying in the bed going through a big pile of jewelry, and she was trying on all the rings. She told my mother, "Shirley, come get you a couple of these rings. Just look through this jewelry and see if there's anything in here you like."

My mother just said, "Did those come in the offering tonight?"

The evangelist's wife said, "Yeah." Mom answered, "No, thank you."

"What are you saying?" asked the evangelist's wife. "Do you see something wrong with that?"

My mother told her, "Yes, there is something wrong with that. The people who gave that jewelry gave it to God. They gave it to the ministry."

"Well, I'm the minister's wife."

"But they didn't give it for you to put on your finger," my mother said. "They gave it to you to sell it, and to put the proceeds back into the ministry." Then she said, "I won't steal from the Lord."

Mom and Dad were fired on the spot, but it didn't matter to them. It was time to move on. They had lost their job and source of livelihood, but they kept their integrity. It wasn't the first time that they had sacrificed all to preserve integrity. It was time to go back home and rebuild their lives again.

All of the life examples my parents plugged in to me as a kid helped me walk the straight and narrow, even during my shaky days. They are part of the reason that, even during that time I came closest to losing my integrity, I didn't. I was in the middle of a test and a messy transition. Once again, as I did at the age of 19, I began questioning everything I believed in. I knew I had a lot of potential, but there was a certain restlessness inside me that I didn't know how to handle.

I was about to learn firsthand that if you do things with a pure heart, even if you are so confused that you take a wrong turn here or there, then God will meet you where you are at. If you cry out to Him with a pure heart, "God, I am confused. I'm trying to be honest instead of just glossing things over," then you can be sure that He will hear you and answer your prayer. Just don't plan on clocking the speed of His answer with a stopwatch. God moves in His own time according to His own agenda. One thing is for sure, though: God always moves *on time.*

I left Christ's Church on the premise, "It's just not time for me to do this anymore. It is time for me to move on. I don't hate anybody; it's just time to go." After that I went through a year of tough times while I tried to establish and build up my own production company. I can tell you today that the struggle was worth it, but at the time I might have mumbled some other answer. I learned a lot while I was at Christ Church, but I knew that if I wanted to grow any further, I had to take the next step in God.

Missions: A New Love

One experience that had a life-changing effect on me was my first trip to Russia in 1990 with Dale Yerton. It transformed my character and worldview, and it helped move me to another phase of searching in my life. This was my first trip out of the States. We went to Moscow and hardly anywhere else, but it was an eye-opener. I wouldn't say that my first trip there was very fruitful, but it did whet my appetite for the foreign mission field. Like many Pentecostal kids, I had always felt a romance toward the mission field—perhaps even a destiny for it. But I had never had a chance to find out if I really liked it.

My first trip to Russia answered that question: I really loved it. I also went to South Africa with Dale Yerton in 1991, and that sharpened my appetite for foreign missions even more. Then in March of 1993, I made my first trip to the Ukraine, a republic formerly under the Soviet system, which bordered the Black Sea, Poland, and Russia. This time I went with some seasoned people who spoke the language and had a full-time office operating in the Ukraine. They knew how to get in and out of the country, and they arranged to send us on a music tour of the nation. That is when I saw the hunger of the people.

I ministered along with a soloist named Deneen Alexandrow Turner, a Baptist woman who was raised in Florida by her Ukrainian mother and Russian father. She spoke English, Russian, and Ukrainian fluently. Deneen was attached to Christ Church and that is where I got to know her and her husband, Mark Turner. She has a tremendous burden for her people, and she made the first Christian record ever recorded in the Ukraine.

Dan Scott, the associate pastor, was the one who urged me to accompany Deneen on a missions trip to the Ukraine. It wasn't a hard sell. I had always had a soft heart toward missions anyway, and his descriptions of missions work really made me excited. When I heard Deneen share her burden for the Ukrainian people, I knew I had to go.

The Ukraine was the bread basket or the "Kansas" of the former USSR, but it is very much the opposite of Russia in its culture and priorities. When Stalin's forces overran the Ukraine, an effort was made to do away with the unique culture and traditions of its people, but they are a very tough people. They are fighters. Their culture is very much intact today.

We played to packed houses of 2,000 or more throughout the 12-day tour, and we took every opportunity to sow the seed of the gospel. Several months earlier, Deneen had single-handedly put up a public Christmas tree in Moscow's Red Square—the first ever to be put up under the Communist leadership of the Soviet Union. It towered 80 feet above Red Square, and Deneen did it with a corporate sponsorship from Coca-Cola! She also bought presents to give away, and won corporate sponsorship to send in truckloads of dolls and toys as a humanitarian effort to needy children in the Moscow area. Then she led the crowd in singing Christmas carols around this Christmas tree in the shadow of the Kremlin!

To make a long story short, I absolutely fell in love with the Ukrainian people. Oddly enough, they fell in love with me too (much to my surprise). I loved Europe. While we were still there, we did the preliminary leg work for a choir tour in June of 1993. I assisted Deneen as she handled every arrangement from transportation to visas to customs to arranging for sound gear in the Ukraine (which can *really* be a challenge). To my delight, the Ukrainians immediately felt comfortable working with me, and they even trusted me (they normally don't trust anybody). Somehow the Lord let me intuitively understand their culture, which should have been impossible.

God connected us with a man who, although we weren't sure he was a Christian at the time, had opened his heart to help us. He taught in a number of universities there, and he had high connections. We were allowed to do a tour when it was against the law to do so because of all the shortages. He got us buses when nobody else could get them; he got us into concert halls and made sound systems appear out of nowhere—when anyone else would have had a hard time finding a meal, let alone a concert site. I loved it.

The more I went to the Ukraine, the less I wanted to come back home. I saw the potential of the Ukraine as an untapped market for the gospel (although in the eighth and ninth centuries the Ukraine had been a hotbed of revival and Christian fervor despite persecution and opposition). My spirit soared when I was told the story of Prince Vladimir, a Ukrainian prince who ruled from Kiev, which is the Ukrainian seat of government to this day. Prince Vladimir had an incurable disease, but one day an evangelist came to Kiev preaching the Kingdom of God (probably some time in the ninth century). This evangelist told everybody to repent, and he told the prince, and all the rulers of Kiev, "If you will repent and bow before the Lord, and if you will let me baptize you, the Lord will heal your incurable disease." Prince Vladimir repented and was baptized, and the Lord instantly healed him. When that happened, thousands of Ukrainians followed their prince and were baptized. Kiev was made a Christian city, and the Ukraine was considered a Christian nation.

All this ties in to my three-year wandering period in Nashville for this reason: When I went to the Ukraine, I felt alive. When I was home, I felt like I was *entertaining* a church with a choir and arrangements (although the truth is that Christ Church has more than its share of true disciples and seekers of God). But when I was in the Ukraine, I was *ministering* life to hungry people. This experience in the Ukraine was an eye-opener that exerted incredible influence over my emotions and thoughts. It showed me a world that was much smaller than I had been led to believe, and yet it was huge in the sense that there is so much to do for the Kingdom of God. There were people out there who actually wanted to hear the truth. I sometimes felt like many American believers had to have things candy-coated or heated "just right" before they would receive it.

I may have been a bit hard on the good people at Christ Church in my thinking in those days, but I couldn't help the way I felt. I was fighting a losing battle against cynicism, and it nearly caused me to abandon all my Pentecostal roots. If you are in the same place today, it is important to separate the actions and sins of men from the truth and purposes of God. Men will always tend to fall short of God's best, just because they are human. But that is no reason to abandon God's plans and purposes for the abundant life.

The best part of this story—and the best thing I can tell you at this point in the book—is that God never left me or abandoned me. He was there all the time, quietly guiding my steps toward the destiny He had ordained for me, despite my feelings of overwhelming confusion and unhappiness. I have news for you too: God will never leave you either. He will never abandon you. It is no accident that you are reading these words today; it is part of His gentle prodding and leading to take you from "here" to "there."

If you seek Him with a pure heart, then no matter how many wrong turns you've taken or how many pitfalls you've discovered, you are in line for a touch of glory, a divine visitation that will sovereignly answer your questions, calm your fears, and establish your steps. All it takes is a touch from God.

Chapter 6

The Cry of My Heart on Overhill Drive

I used to say that the hardest thing I ever did was resign from my job at Christ Church. In my heart I knew it was time to go, even though my head told me that it was the stupidest thing I had ever done. Everything was going well and everyone treated me well. We had just put out a record that was winning some national success and people were starting to think, *Well, that Cooley guy isn't too bad at what he does.* But when the Lord said, "Leave," I left.

I spent the next year trying to build my business as a studio musician and independent producer in Nashville. The funny thing is that in my heart I really didn't want to be a studio musician. I would go do those dates and get ulcers. I didn't really want to do it but the Lord allowed me to because I said I wanted to. Then I began to think, *Well, maybe I don't have the ability.*

One of my dearest friends, Gary Lunn, is a session bass player in Nashville. I asked him, "Gary, do you think I have what it takes to play in a studio? Do you think I really have it?" He said, "Lindell, you're phenomenal. You can do anything you want to do. Just spend a few days with a drum machine and get back in sync with your metronome and you can do anything you want." But still I didn't want to.

You see, the Lord was saying to me, "Yes, you can do this, but *this is not what I want you to do.* You can have this, but there are a couple of pieces of food over here on some plates that you haven't dug into yet. That is what I want you to have, but you keep wanting all this other stuff first." It wasn't surprising that every time I would get something I thought I needed, I wouldn't want it. God wanted me to desire the things He wanted in my life, but He had to take me through a process of breaking. God knew how high the stakes would be, how many souls would be on the line beginning in the summer of 1995.

Lord, Are You Still There?

The Lord blessed me with a lot of work until I reached the three-month period from June to August of 1994, when I almost starved to death.

Everything seemed to shut down on me. My bills were falling behind and everything was looking bad and getting worse. Then I thought, "I'll call Dad. He'll help me." That was on a day when things were at their worst. Suddenly something rose up inside me. I put my feet on the floor of my bedroom, rolled out of bed, and made a declaration out loud to my empty room:

"You know what, God? This is between You and me. This has nothing to do with my dad. I believe that You called me when I was a little boy. If You indeed called me, then You can provide for me. If I'm being disobedient in some area, You can show it to me. But I'll starve before I call anybody for help. I will not ask for anything. It's not because I'm prideful. But until You tell me to do that, I'm not going to do it. I'm going to trust You."

I was as stubborn as a mule, but this time God was using it for good. My crisis hit in October or November, and I decided to walk up Overhill Drive where I lived in Nashville to get some coffee. I had a favorite coffee shop nearby where I always went to read the paper, think, and study. As I walked up the hill the tears just kept coming—it was beyond my control. I had just offered a prayer that was really the cry of my heart to the Lord. I had hit bottom and the Lord was my only way out, but my prayer just wasn't finished yet...

"Lord, the only thing I want is this: I want to know You. I've seen a lot of religion, from the tent revivals on to the churches. I've seen men who were men of God and I've seen some shysters. I've seen young kids come here to Nashville with a desire to be something for the Lord. And I've seen that desire taken right out of them—suddenly they want 'a career.' Lord, I just want to know You."

I kept walking up Overhill Drive and the tears kept flowing down my face. I gave up trying to wipe them away. Evidently the Spirit wasn't finished with me, because from the depths of my being I cried out to the Lord right there in the street,

> *"Lord, I have worked in great churches and I have been out traveling on weekends to minister in churches, and I can count on one hand how many people I've seen saved in the past few years. Is it that You just don't want to save sinners anymore?*

> *"God, if You're still real, do You still heal people without medicine? Now, I know You often heal through medicine and the knowledge You have given us, but I'm asking if You still do it without medical help? Do You still deliver people from homosexuality? From drug addiction and substance abuse without the aid of Alcoholics Anonymous or anything else? Can You still do that—or was that ever You?"*

I hadn't seen God do something miraculous for so long that I was beginning to think maybe these things were just fond memories from my childhood that I had "waxed over with honey." I seriously wondered if I'd somehow made my childhood memories better than they really were. Was I just remembering an ideal picture of God's power like it never really was? Is it possible that it was never really like that? I'll never forget my final cry on Overhill Drive that day:

> *"Lord, if You still do these things, will You please put me where it's at? I'm tired of imitation Christianity. I'm tired of having great music, and watching people come out to get good, warm, fuzzy feelings. I want to see You—I want to see You shake people and mow them down and do it right. Change them. Let them come out as soldiers."*

I knew I had prayed an honest prayer, but I didn't realize then how powerful it was. The Church is praying the same kind of prayer all across the world today. Believers across America particularly are crying out, "God, lift us out of this pit of hypocrisy. Is there anything real? Dear Lord, is there anything more to this than the country club mentality?"

The Next Step

From that day on my business picked up. I just got busier and busier producing albums and traveling on weekends to do choir clinics and preach. I was so busy that I had to start turning down customers and ministry requests.

One of the first things that happened after the long drought was that I was offered a job as music minister with one of the largest churches in the country. This high-profile ministry had daily national television exposure and the ability to pay me well for my labors, and the pastor wanted me to take the lead position.

I flew up north where the church was located and interviewed for the job, but before I left I jotted down 29 things I would have to have to ever be a music director again. When I sat down with this pastor and read the list to him, he said, "We would be crazy to consider someone with these requirements. I can't do this." Then he called me back later and said, "We have reconsidered this, and we'll agree to your requests. We want you to come." I told him, "Brother, I need to apologize to you. I knew those requirements were ridiculous when I wrote them. I am blessed that you have reconsidered your decision and that you want me to come, but I know I don't belong there. I'd love to take it, but I know I'm not the man for the job."

I went to the interview because I really was interested, but there were two things working against my taking the job. The first was the influence of the Holy Spirit, who knew what lay ahead of me in just a matter of months. The second wasn't so good, but this was the influence that I knew about at the time. In my mind, I felt that when I left Christ Church that I had "graduated" to "real ministry."

I had bought the lie that is perpetuated in the church world by pastors and music ministers alike. I felt like a second-class musician citizen, a hireling subcontractor to be hired and fired at will with little regard to calling or anointing. I longed for the respect that went with being a "real minister" instead of being chained to the piano for life and being treated like a perpetual teenager.

The idea of willingly stepping back under what I saw as a yoke of bondage as a music minister was revolting to me. I was now an up and coming music producer, businessman, and traveling minister. It would take a lot for me to give it all up for a church job again. It was this kind of thinking that fueled my list of 29 points. It involved matters of respect, reasonable work schedules not tied to a time clock or strictly daylight hours (since much of a music minister's work takes place in endless evening choir and band rehearsals and writing music charts at home), and reasonable pay.

Unfortunately, my list of 29 points was almost guaranteed to offend the average pastor. (We will deal extensively with pastor/musician relationships in a later chapter.) If you think this shows that I had an attitude problem, you are right. God was working overtime to completely overhaul my life priorities, and in the end it would take a touch of His glory to complete the work.

The Ties to Brownsville

In September of 1994, one month after my job interview up north, I was in Navarre, Florida, just a few miles from Pensacola. Dale and Evelyn Yerton, some missionary friends, had called me about producing a record for them. Like most missionaries, they couldn't afford to do a record in Nashville. Even a simple project would have cost $10,000 at that time. So I told them, "I know of some folks down in Florida who do great records at a really reasonable price." They said, "That sounds good, but will you produce it for us? We have never been in a studio before." I told them, "Sure!" despite my packed schedule. Something in my heart said that they really needed the help and that I really needed to do it for them.

So I flew to Pensacola and drove over to Navarre to meet Dale and Evelyn. I didn't know it, but Dale was scheduled to preach that Wednesday night at an Assembly of God church in Brownsville pastored by John Kilpatrick, and I went along with them to the service.

This was the second time I'd met John Kilpatrick. After the service we all went out to a particular oyster restaurant in Pensacola, and there was something oddly familiar about that place. Then I remembered it.

In 1985, I'd played piano for Rusty Goodman when he ministered at Brownsville Assembly of God (but I didn't meet Pastor Kilpatrick then). I did remember coming to that exact oyster restaurant for dinner, however. That place had the best soft-shelled crab I'd ever had.

Then three years later in 1988, I came down to Pensacola with my parents just to get away from North Alabama for a few days. I remember my dad saying, "I want to go to church on Wednesday night. I've been wanting to hear John Kilpatrick preach. I've got some of his tapes and he is a good preacher."

So we went to Brownsville Assembly and heard Pastor Kilpatrick preach. He was preaching a sermon about the need for caution about the book that was the rage in 1988 called, *Eighty-Eight Reasons Why the Lord Is Coming in 1988*. I remember that the service was held in what is now the chapel across the street. I didn't talk to John Kilpatrick that night, but my dad did. After the service, you probably know what we did. We went to that same oyster restaurant and ordered soft-shelled crab.

I enjoyed Dale's ministry at Brownsville Assembly in September of 1994, and once again we all went to that oyster restaurant after the service. I remember that

John Kilpatrick kept looking at me and kept asking me questions and trying to maintain a conversation. I asked him my usual question, "Well, how about your music guy?" I had a habit of checking out the pastors I met to see how they treated their music people. Many pastors treat ministers of music or worship leaders like a necessary evil, and only a few feel like they are true ministers.

I can still remember Pastor Kilpatrick's reply. His comments about his music minister were so good that I was really impressed with him. He and Brenda, his wife, said, "We love Tom. Tom is the best there is—there is nobody better." And, as always, the soft-shelled crab was incredible. I was really getting to like that restaurant. I had been told that it was a family restaurant, and that the whole family got involved in the act. I couldn't help but think back then, *That must be some family.*

One month later, in October of 1994, I saw John Kilpatrick again at a missions conference held by a group called Worldwide Missionary Evangelism. It was a good, solid fellowship composed of a small number of men who shared a common vision for world missions. I didn't know it, but John Kilpatrick was scheduled to preach in the day services. (The reason that I came to their conference was because they had never asked me to do anything. They simply wanted me to come and enjoy.) My contact with John consisted of a brief hello and good-bye. Yet it served the important purpose of planting me in John's memory for another time.

"I'm Not Interested"

When I jumped into 1995, I had project after project lined up and all the budgets were high enough that it looked like I was actually going to make a really good living. The downside to it all was that with my coming out of the two challenging years at Christ Church, and then going through a grueling year establishing my own production company and going from church to church doing seminars and preaching, I was exhausted.

Right in the middle of all this, John Kilpatrick called me in Nashville in February of 1995. He said, "Lindell, Tom has resigned. I picked up the phone three times to call you and slammed it back down because I thought, *Oh, Lindell won't do it.* But Lindell, the Lord spoke to me and told me that you are supposed to be in Pensacola."

The silence must have been deafening. Even though I had cried out to the Lord from my heart, I was living and working in the very cynical showbiz city of Nashville. Anytime someone in Nashville says, "The Lord" anything, you generally write him or her off as a little weird, or manipulative at best. My answer was anything but warm and positive.

"John, either you or the Lord has missed it. I'll give you one guess as to which one it is. You see, I never want to be a music director ever again in my life. I strictly will not do it."

Pastor Kilpatrick's call had triggered all the things I had been wrestling with for three years. My mind was racing with statements like, *I was called to preach when I was 17, and I am actively working in the foreign missions field. Yes, I did music, but now is my time to preach, it is not time to do music. God called me to preach, and I need to preach, not be somebody's piano player.* The bottom line was that I felt like it would be one giant step backwards for me to be a music minister again.

John Kilpatrick calmly replied, "Well, I tell you what we'll do—I know when God speaks to me. So will you do me a favor?" he asked.

"What?"

"Will you pray for three days?"

"I'll pray for three days," I said, "because I know that I have no desire." Then John asked me a question I could really bite into. He said, "Well, what do you think about Pensacola?"

"Do you want the truth? It's hot and humid and I hate it." (What an interview.) I said, "I love the mountains and I love the streams. That's me."

That was on a Sunday afternoon. On Monday morning, I got up and grudgingly said a prayer that sounded something like this: "Lord, You really don't want me to go to Pensacola, do You? I didn't think so." I told myself I was keeping the letter of my word to Pastor Kilpatrick.

I hadn't promised him that I would pray a nice, open prayer—and he definitely didn't get it. All I offered to God was a closed, nailed-down prayer to match my mood. I would soon find out that I had grossly underestimated John Kilpatrick and the God who spoke to him.

John Kilpatrick called me back on Monday and said, "I'm coming to Nashville tomorrow night. Will you have dinner with me?" I said, "Yeah, John, but man, I'm not interested—*really*." John didn't flinch. He just said, "I'm supposed to have dinner with you." What could I say at that point? I was beginning to learn that there was just no way to tell this man "no" once he has heard from the Lord. I had another major lesson just ahead of me.

Chapter 7

The Offer I Was Determined to Refuse

I picked up Pastor John Kilpatrick at his hotel at ten o'clock in the evening and took him to dinner. I gave in to the ornery side of my nature and decided to take John to a restaurant on the trendy side of Nashville where all the musicians hang out late at night. It gets kind of weird there at night because of the characters who wander in there when the moon comes out.

My hair was real long at that point, and I have to confess that I was thinking, *You know, John Kilpatrick leans a bit to the conservative side. Now I've seen him before, and he always wears a tie and coat, every hair is in place, and his shoes are always polished up. I'm going to blow him out of the water so that he won't want me to work with him.* (I was absolutely wrong to have that kind of attitude, of course.)

Just before John arrived, I had dug out the legal pad with the infamous list of 29 points I had developed for the job interview up north. My first surprise came when I met John Kilpatrick in the hotel lobby. He had been converted. There wasn't a single tie, dress shirt, dress jacket, or polished leather dress shoe in sight. The man was dressed casually and he looked relaxed (but every hair was still in place, as short as it was).

When we reached the restaurant, I took my legal pad with "the terrible 29" into the restaurant with me and laid it down on a chair beside me, reminding myself, *I don't want this job. I don't want to do this. I'm burned. I'm sick of this. I just want to go to the mission field and stay there.* I hadn't told anybody yet, but I was thinking about moving to the Ukraine to work full-time as a resident missionary with some people I'd been working with on a part-time basis for six years.

At that time, I was convinced that nothing could save the United States, and that our society was going to hell in a hand basket. (Of course, many Christians still think this way today, but once I experienced the life-changing power of God in the revival, my opinions changed permanently.) I had an absolutely nasty attitude toward churches and pastors and everything else in general except the Ukraine.

When John first told me that I was supposed to come to Pensacola as his minister of music, I first envisioned a big church with an "IBM employee-type set-up," which I despised. You can get that impression when you first meet John Kilpatrick, because he is so immaculate, self-controlled, and self-assured. What I didn't realize was that Pastor Kilpatrick is also very artistic. He has a very creative flair, and he understands the creative mind very well.

So John and I sat down across from each other at this restaurant, surrounded by the best and the worst that Nashville nightlife has to offer. Then Pastor Kilpatrick looked up at me from his menu, and the first thing he said was, "I really like your hair." Now that really threw me off balance. This man just refused to stay in the box I'd put him in. Then he threw me off again when we ordered food. I had figured all along that the food this place offered would really turn him off, but John said that he loved the food.

If that wasn't bad enough, John started telling me things I *never* expected to hear from him. He started in by saying, "Lindell, here's what I want you to do. Now I want you to do this, this, this, and this, this, this." I was glancing over at my list so I would be prepared once he started in about my coming to Pensacola, but I never had the opportunity to say a thing. The man might as well have been reading directly from my 29-point list! I'm telling you that John Kilpatrick was rattling off every item on my "guaranteed to offend a pastor list"! Even worse, *he was doing it **in order**: one, two, three, four, five, six....* . What was I going to do now? John Kilpatrick had beat me to the punch by offering me everything on the list—*in order.*

By the time Pastor Kilpatrick got to item number ten, I just looked at him and said, "You're not serious?!

I mean, John, come on! Nobody, and I mean nobody, wants anybody to work on those terms. At least not any pastor I know. Come on. You're out of your mind! You're off your rocker."

"No," he said. "This is what I want." What I didn't realize is that John has a great deal of wisdom. Sure, he is a human being like anybody else, but Pastor Kilpatrick has a supernatural gift of wisdom. He knows how to deal with people, and he is no dummy. He knew that I didn't want the job, and the Lord showed him why. Then God gave him every point on my list—in order. When John started going down my list, he was taking away all my crutches and carefully crafted reasons to say no—even before I could open my mouth!

No More Options

Well, by the time he got all the way down to the money part at "item number 29," I didn't care what he said. God had supernaturally taken away my options. The choice had already been made and sealed. I got up from that table knowing that I was coming to Pensacola. I didn't tell him I would. I just said something religious like, "Well, I'll pray about it," but I knew that I was coming. I would have come even if he said I had to work for free, because I had discovered who the real Architect was behind this deal. I had asked God to do something and He was doing it, whether I was ready or not.

I remember telling my friends in the music business, "I am getting ready to do the stupidest thing I have

ever done in my life—I'm going to move to Pensacola."
I still remember one friend telling me, "Lindell, that is
absolutely the stupidest thing I've ever heard of." He
said, "You know, Lindell, you are just now getting to
where people will use you. This is stupid."

I knew what he was talking about. There is a saying
among the musicians, engineers, and producers
around Nashville that goes, "If you ever leave town,
forget it." Once you leave, you are considered gone
and forgotten; out of sight, out of mind. Everyone in
the business had told me from the beginning, "Lindell,
you have to stay in there and work at it. Don't ever
leave town and live somewhere else and expect to
come back. You'll have to start all over again from the
bottom."

None of that mattered once I heard John Kilpatrick
rattle off my "terrible 29." There was only one way that
man could have come up with that list, and His name
has three letters. We set a time in February for me to
fly to Pensacola so I could try out for the job and everything seemed to go well—despite my long hair. I was
right about one thing—the church was immaculate
and everything was in its proper place, just like its pastor. After the service, I went out for dinner with the
Kilpatricks to that same oyster restaurant I liked so
much. They introduced me to the Linkenhoker family,
the owners of the restaurant. I found out that it indeed
was a large family and that they attended Brownsville
Assembly of God. I dimly remember a pretty daughter

who seemed shy at the time, and our greeting consisted of a quick "hello, good-bye."

What About Toronto?

I must have made the cut at the tryout because John called me and asked if I could move to Pensacola in time to minister for the Palm Sunday morning service on April 9, 1995. From February until April, John Kilpatrick and I talked on the phone almost every day. Our hearts were hungry for more of the Lord. Our conversations turned toward revival again and again. "What do you think about Toronto? What do you suppose is going on there?" We both grew tired of answering, "I don't know," since we both *wanted* to know. We had read articles, both pro and con, about it, and we had our own questions, but in the end we both agreed: "Something has to be going on for people to be touched like that."

Finally, John called me one day and said, "Brenda and a sister in my church are going up to Toronto. I can't get away, so I'm sending them there in my place. Now, Brenda and I have been married for 26 years and I can guarantee you that she is a no-nonsense lady. She will know in a minute if it isn't real."

Brenda returned a few days later, changed. Her hunger for the Lord was so intensified, she could barely keep from continual worship and prayer. Therefore, John planned to make a trip around the end of March and called me to see if I wanted to go with him and some others. I told him, "I'll tell you what. I'll call my dad. He would like to go too." So I called up Dad and we all went to Toronto. Well, most of us did. Pastor got as far as Chattanooga and was diverted.

We arrived and soon found out that John Arnott and the main pastoral staff were ministering in Europe. It wasn't long before I found myself critical of the music, the sound system, everything. The pastor filling in from a Vineyard church in California delivered a very, very simple sermon. He ended with an equally laid back invitation for prayer. He said, "You know, if you guys here, if you want to come and receive prayer, uhhh, just come on up and you'll see tape on the floor. Just, uh, put your toes on the tape and then wait, and somebody will be by to pray with you. If the front is full, then go to the back."

Oh, My Pentecostal Pride

I started toward the front, but when I saw that it was full I headed to the back. The meeting facility is very large, and the very back of the auditorium has a low ceiling with fluorescent lights and row after row of tape on the rug. You couldn't hear the music at all because the music team was way up in the front. It was like being out in the foyer of a large church or auditorium. There were no speakers overhead and no chairs on the floor, and the only ambiance was provided by the cold, hard fluorescent lights buzzing overhead.

I went back there, toed the line, and began to pray. I had lifted my hands up in the good old Pentecostal way (using the familiar "I surrender" stance). The first guy who came by to pray for me took it upon himself to show me that I was doing it wrong. He told me that I should put my hands in more of a "receiving mode." So I had to flip my hands over, which irritated me.

I remember standing there with my toes obediently lined up on that tape thinking, *What a fool you are. Lindell, you have turned into a charismatic zealot. You are going to bounce off the wall!* I didn't want to admit it at the time, but sometimes Pentecostals can exhibit a lot of arrogance. We like to remind anyone who will listen, "Well, we Pentecostals knew about the Spirit of God long before all these Baptists and Methodists ever got in on it." I confess that I felt that spiritual pride rising up when I was having my hands "readjusted" for proper reception. *What am I, a TV antenna?* I thought. I could almost hear myself saying, "I know better than this. I've seen people walk out of wheelchairs in my life. What am I doing here?"

When the guy prayed for me, he said something like, "Oh, Lord, I just ask You just to touch him right now. Just give him more of You, more of Your glory." And I felt nothing. Later on I would realize that the lack of results probably had nothing to do with the man praying for me or with his prayer. The problem was the prayee. If you were God, would you bless an arrogant Pentecostal with more of what he is already prideful about?

As the evening wore on, my cynicism wore on me too. Then I saw my dad coming toward me from the front where he had been helping with the ministry. "Son, come here," he said. "Look at this lady. She's got the glory of God." Now Dad is an old-timer in the things of the Spirit, and he can recognize the move of the Holy Spirit in a split second.

The policy there at the time was that you could "catch" in the prayer line if you were a pastor—even though you were just a visitor. The leadership invited all the visiting pastors and ministers to come up and help catch and Dad obliged. When he motioned me over, I thought, *Here I am going to catch, and I don't even know if I believe in it.* I grew up believing that if you were really slain in the Spirit, if it was *really* God, then it wouldn't hurt you to fall. I thought that you only needed catchers for fakers, if you know what I mean. I was about to be shown a more perfect way.

When Dad and I got to about the third person in line, we noticed her start to tremble. In that instant, I felt the fire of God come on me too! All of a sudden I started crying. I still didn't have any other kind of a manifestation or anything—I just cried. When I finally lifted my eyes, the missionary inside of me suddenly saw a room full of people from all over the world seeking God. I thought, *God, something is up. You're doing something in the world.* God's glory affected us so much that my dad and I would go back to our room after each service and just cry and cry. When Dad talked to my mother on the phone he cried. We would just weep over people in compassion during our four-day stay in Toronto, but other than that there wasn't anything wild happening to us.

When I returned to Nashville on Friday I had to pack up everything for the move to Pensacola that Saturday night. I had hired movers to help me do the packing and there were boxes everywhere. I had never bought any Vineyard music in my life, but the first thing I did when I got back in Nashville was to go out and buy a Vineyard worship CD. I used to dislike Vineyard music because I didn't think it had any get-up-and-go or fire in it. If I heard it being played on a friend's stereo or in a church, I would think, *This is so lazy. When is this music going to get somewhere?* I kind of characterized it as laid-back California beach music, and I wasn't from California or the beach.

A Final Breaking

My experience with God in Toronto did something so powerful in me that it even changed my music tastes—in a radical way. All of a sudden I couldn't get enough "California beach music" from Vineyard. God was teaching me the contemplative, worshipful side of prayer and worship. There was a song written by Kelly Carpenter on one of the Vineyard albums called, "Draw Me Close." The first verse goes, "Draw me close to You/Never let me go," and the chorus says, "You're all I want/You're all I've ever needed/You're all I want/Help me know You are near."[1] I played "Draw Me Close" over and over. I put it on the repeat mode in my CD player and played it over and over—and cried.

I don't know what those movers thought that weekend. There I was walking through rooms crammed with boxes with those movers who probably weren't Christians at all. They were in there wrestling with boxes and furniture and just cussing away—while I cried. I think one of them asked me, "Are you okay?" and I managed to get out an answer between sobs, "Yeah, I'm all right."

Part of the cause for my weeping dealt with a final breaking God was doing in my heart. I wasn't just packing boxes for a move. I was burning some bridges that it had taken me a good chunk of my lifetime to build. I was going to become a music minister at a relatively unknown Assembly of God church in Pensacola, Florida, and my head and emotions still didn't want to do it. It was difficult to pack at times that weekend because I knew full well that I was kissing my dream, my baby, my pet, good-bye. My "pet" was my recently successful career as a Nashville producer. I had accumulated about $70,000 worth of recording gear and some invaluable contacts in the industry. I had just produced Karen Wheaton's latest record and landed some more Christian projects with significant budgets. I knew that I was kissing the music business good-bye, and it wasn't easy. I had staked a lot of my identity and personal self-esteem on my accomplishments in that industry. God said let it go, leave it behind, and don't look back once you've set your hand to the plow. The breaking was final. There was no turning back.

The real fruit of change showed up immediately in my leading worship at Brownsville Assembly of God. I started singing some of the Vineyard choruses I had recently come to love, and the Lord did such a work in me that I didn't want to do any black gospel. Now I'm not saying that black gospel is wrong, or less anointed than any other music form. God knew that I was lopsided. I used to major on black gospel and "music with a kick" exclusively while turning my nose up at anything that didn't have a strong beat or syncopation. I was so resigned to what the Lord had done in me in a gentle way, that I thought, *I don't need all that hype music.* I had always needed it before to praise, but I didn't need it anymore. God's touch made me want to bypass praise and jump right into worship. The next phase of God's work in me brought balance to me and to the worship of the Brownsville Revival.

From the day God touched me in April 1995, my life was changed. I arrived in Pensacola and found out that everyone who had gone to Toronto was starving to death for God's glory like I was. You see, the revival didn't break out in Brownsville just because Lindell Cooley arrived, and it didn't break out just because a bunch of us went to Toronto. Although many people in the Brownsville congregation had been pouring themselves into fervent intercession for years, nothing seemed to be punching through. We didn't know it then, but revival wouldn't break until about two months later. When it came, it came because God decided to visit His people in His time. However, I do believe that the Lord allowed many of us to experience a foretaste of His glory in other places. Every one of us wanted *a touch of His glory* and nothing else would do anymore.

We began to gather together as a staff on Pastor Kilpatrick's back porch to seek God and pray for each other. It was there that God first began to visit us with His glory, and we would sometimes bask in His presence until two or three in the morning. Yet no matter what we did or how hard we prayed, it just would not spread to the main service. Since John Kilpatrick is not the type to force the issue, we waited.

Endnote

1. "Draw Me Close" written by Kelly Carpenter, Copyright 1994 Mercy/Vineyard Publishing, reproduced by permission. Note: This song later appeared on a Pensacola worship album recorded live at the revival and produced by Vineyard Music in 1995 entitled, *Winds of Worship 7: Live from Brownsville.*

Chapter 8

The Glory
Comes Suddenly

One of the most important things I can tell you is
that true revival comes when God descends upon man
in His glory. That's it. There is no formula or religious
dogma to memorize and implement at your church.
There is no "12-Step Revival Plan in a Can" that you
can purchase at some expensive church growth semi-
nar. Extraordinary things happen when the Extraordinary God shows up among ordinary people who long
for more of Him. That is a summary of what happened
at Brownsville Assembly of God on Father's Day in
June of 1995.

When I moved my mountain of boxes to Pensacola,
Florida, and began to lead worship there, I quickly realized that I had come to an ordinary Assemblies of God
church. Pastor John Kilpatrick was a wonderful pastor
and a skilled teacher of the Word, but he struggled

with the same problems every other pastor has to deal with. He worried about motivating and training workers, finding time to handle his counseling load, and balancing his roles as administrator, family man, and spiritual leader of the flock. He worried about the welfare of the sheep in his care, and he was fervently praying for revival. It was a church that wanted more because it didn't have it yet.

I inherited a great worship team and a talented group of musicians, but like anyone else I struggled with rehearsal schedules, motivation problems, and the constant need to learn new songs and resuscitate the old ones. The congregation was a normal mix of young, old, and in-betweens, representing almost every musical taste you could think of. In the midst of the normal challenges, we desperately wanted to see revival spark in our services and we were frustrated. Brownsville Assembly of God was like most of the medium-sized Pentecostal and Charismatic churches scattered across America. We wanted something that we didn't have, and we were pressing in by faith to see it come to pass.

I was scheduled to return to the Ukraine for a short missions trip in June, but before I left I began to teach the worship team, the choir, and the music team some Vineyard worship choruses. I had done away with most of the hard-driving, lively praise songs I favored before. I didn't want to do anything that smacked of hype or emotional manipulation. I just wanted to go directly into worship and bypass praise

altogether. The congregation seemed to enjoy some of
the choruses and was indifferent to others. Something
was still missing.

Revival!

I went to the Ukraine in June of 1995 to help conduct a short choir tour and planned to return the week
after Father's Day. I was getting ready to leave the
Ukraine when revival came "suddenly" to the Brownsville congregation on Sunday, June 17th. At the end of
the Father's Day service, the visiting evangelist named
Stephen Hill gave an altar call. He had just delivered a
normal sermon during a normal Sunday service, but
everything changed when the Spirit of God suddenly
descended on the congregation.

Many people who were present, including Pastor
Kilpatrick, literally felt a wind sweep through the sanctuary during the visitation. A thousand people rushed
to the altar that day to confess their sins, repent, and
commit themselves to the Lord without hesitation or
compromise. At this writing, the revival has continued
week after week for two years and 125,000 souls have
been added to the Kingdom by conservative count.
The Lord continues to visit us with ever-increasing
power and glory month after month.

I flew into John F. Kennedy Airport in New York on
Tuesday the 19th after reluctantly bidding my beloved
Ukrainian friends good-bye. I found a phone and im-
mediately called Pastor Kilpatrick.

"Hey, John, what's going on?"

"Lindell, it has happened!"

"What has happened?"

"Revival is here."

I had waited to hear those words for a long time.

My heart leapt in my chest because I knew it had to be real or the man on the other end of the line wouldn't say it like that. I wanted to get back to Pensacola just that much quicker, but I knew I couldn't make it until Wednesday. During the flight from New York to Florida, my mind kept taking me back to those "gentle laid-back moments in God's presence" that I had embraced since April.

When I arrived John and Brenda Kilpatrick picked me up at the airport, and he began to share with me what God was doing. It sounded wonderful, but I was very tired, and felt disconnected. I didn't realize it then, but that disconnected feeling would stay with me for about two weeks. There was no doubt that God was in the house, but I was having trouble entering in. I ran headlong into a major disappointment because I was expecting "Toronto."

Breaking Old Dislikes

First there was this Stephen Hill character. I had never met him before the Wednesday night service after Father's Day, but this evangelist seemed to be just a little "too hyped" for me. Pastor Kilpatrick assured me that he was okay and said that he had known Steve for years. My daydreams of a "gentle" move of the Holy Spirit that morning were jolted back to reality by

Stephen Hill, a dynamo with an unquenchable passion for souls. He was far from gentle. I thought he came across like a speeding freight train that first night.

He had us sing one chorus for 30 minutes straight at a clip of 90 miles an hour, and I felt like I had stepped back into my old Pentecostal roots again. All the wonderful things that the Lord had done for me suddenly seemed to disappear and my own heathenistic self came out again. I thought, *I am not going to do this! Sorry, but I've been there, done that. I don't want to do this! I want that gentle sweetness that I had.*

After the service I was pretty hard on Steve Hill once we were alone. I said, "Steve, I am not going to get up there and do all that hype stuff. If you want it, then get someone else to do it, because I'm not doing it." Frankly, I had a rotten attitude. Do you know what Steve did? He totally disarmed me with his answer. He said, "Well, brother, that's all right. Whatever you want to do." I had to repent to him shortly after that because I was so mean to him. He could have been angry with me but he wasn't. The battles in my heart would continue for a while, but we were on the way to becoming close friends with one heart.

I knew that my reaction to Steve was rooted in my dislike for the old pattern of wanting to be worked up by powerful music. After my breaking in April, I was so moved by the revelation of just loving the Lord that I could be moved to worship at any time by the slightest breath of the Spirit. All I have to do is say from my heart, "Lord God, all You want is my worship. All You want is my attention. You are like a Father to me." I don't need a lengthy time of praise to crank my flesh up to speed. At the mere mention of His name I am ready to fall to my knees and worship. He has touched me so deeply that I must respond.

I didn't realize it, but God was also out to break my deep-seated desire to be somebody important. (Everyone I've ever known has had this desire too.) I was just floating along on a cloud of simply loving Jesus and hungering after the Lord, but there was some hidden poison still lurking in my heart and God wanted it out.

It was the glory of God that finally destroyed the yoke around my neck. Before God touched me, I always thought that God had called me to a greater grace and a higher calling than to just be somebody's "flunky musician." I thank God for His mercy and grace in forgiving my arrogance.

Just when I was convinced that God wasn't doing anything in me, He brought all my wrong motives to the surface. In the first few weeks of the revival, any time Stephen or Pastor Kilpatrick would interrupt one of my songs or stop the worship service to say something, I would be totally offended. I wouldn't say anything or change my actions, but in my spirit I was offended. My face might have been smiling but my heart and head were shouting, "Doggone you, get away from the microphone. I don't interrupt your sermons, do I? Now stay out of my hair—I'm trying to lead worship here." (I am not interested in being "politically correct" in this book; my goal is to speak the truth in love so that you and others can avoid the mistakes I made and move directly into God's best.)

It was wrong, but I felt like these godly men were invading my territory. Musicians seem to have an old link to lucifer the first rebellious worship leader—they have a pride that is never satisfied. They jealously guard what is "theirs" and then wonder why they don't have what the pastor or evangelist has too. God would be using me mightily in worship, and then this "old ugly" would come out. Right then and there, in the middle of an anointed Brownsville Revival service, I would feel my hidden spiritual pride, piety, and ego rise to the surface. I'd catch myself thinking, *I've been in this thing a long time, and here is some old drug addict* [Stephen Hill] preaching a sermon. Dear God, he just said he got saved in 1975! I was rolling on the floor and speaking in tongues in 1975. Why, I've been in church all my life and never veered from the path! (Sounds like the older brother of the Prodigal son, doesn't it?)

God never let me get away with it. He would just zap me and say, "*Stop it. If you want Me, humble yourself.* Yes, you thought you had that jealousy under control, but I brought that out to show you that you don't. Repent of it, and let it go."

One of the greatest joys of working with Pastor John Kilpatrick and Stephen Hill is the fact that they are transparent. They prefer direct communication. I told Pastor John one night after service, "You know, God has brought out some really ugly stuff in me, and

I've had to repent." I don't think he was surprised, but I do know he was pleased.

When the Spirit's work was complete in the area of my calling and self-worth in Christ (He has *so much* more to do in me), I had a totally different attitude. Now any time those brothers need to say something or interrupt for any reason, I think, *That's fine, brother. I trust your judgment. Go ahead and do anything you want to do. If you want to prophesy, if you want to stop me in the middle of my favorite song, that's fine.* Yes, the musician in me will still occasionally grumble a little bit when I'm interrupted, but now I have a tolerance for it. I just tell myself, *Oh well, what is the big deal? The guy is trying to follow the Lord here. Relax.*

Pastor Kilpatrick, Stephen Hill, and I have great confidence in one another today. We trust each other. We've cried and wept in each other's arms, and we are soldiers. We've been in the fox hole together, we've watched out for each other's back, so all of the small differences and irritations just don't bother us now.

New Things—Even in Revival

Once my eyes were opened to the incredible work God was doing in me those first two weeks in revival, I became content. I realized, for the first time in my life, that I wasn't "somebody's" piano player—*I was God's piano player.* (My mother had been saying it for decades, but I guess I just wasn't listening close enough.) If that was what God wanted me to do for the rest of my life, then praise His name; I would be content. I had to pass that hurdle before the other gifts within me could be released to grow. If I had failed to pass that test, my selfish ambitions would have tainted all the other gifts and callings in my life.

Very early in the revival we began to notice some supernatural occurrences in the worship service that let us know God was personally involved in this revival—even in areas not related to the hundreds of souls won each night and the filled altars. I looked in my personal journal and found an entry dated August 17, 1995 (about two months after the revival began). This is what I wrote down after I got home that night:

8-17-95

*The service tonight seemed to be pretty average until the very end. As I was about to leave, I talked with Richard Crisco, the youth pastor, and he questioned me about a particular worship chorus we had sung toward the end of the service. It was an ad lib thing that just came out of the air. He wanted to know how I was able to cue the sound track tape to come in as precisely as it did. I told him **there was no tape**, it was just me and the keyboard—there weren't even any singers, but he didn't believe me. He said that he had heard at least three voices and several instruments.*

As Richard spoke, I remembered that I too had heard a third voice singing a beautiful counter melody, but was so caught up in the presence of the Lord that I didn't see who was singing, or who it might be. I knew I was singing, and I assumed it was Jeff

Oettle [one of the worship singers at the time], or someone who had felt inspired and grabbed the mike to join in.

As Richard talked, I remembered two things: First, the third voice was exceptionally clear, and the counter melody sounded rehearsed. Second, when we had finished singing, I went to sit by Pastor John who was a little lost in the Spirit (in other words, he was out like he always is), and he told me in slurred speech, "That new chorus you just did was wonderful. Could you do it again tomorrow night?"

Later on, Benny Johnson (the sound guy) and Van Lane (the children's pastor) told me that they had heard it too. They were at the sound board, and were trying to find out what channel the third voice was on. [It wasn't going through the sound board at all!]

My conclusion, that the third voice was definitely not of this world, wow.

Later that week I asked Jeff Oettle, "Were you singing with me?"

"No, but I was standing on stage."

Then I asked him, "Did anybody else sing with me?"

I already knew the answer—no.

All this happened during a Thursday night service, and I remember that the entire worship team was exhausted because early in the revival we used to sing for hours at the end. Somewhere close to midnight, the band started to really sound bad and the singers were nearly out of it, so I dismissed them so they could get some rest. I punched in a piano program with a breathy sound on my electronic keyboard, and I just started playing a chord with a monastic Gregorian chant style.

I clearly remember hearing a backup voice and a third voice come in that was singing a perfect counter melody to my song, except that *it wasn't repeating* what I was saying—that would have been impossible anyway. I was making it up as I went. Yet this voice was singing at the same time I was singing in perfect counter melody with an incredibly clear voice.

I was making up the melody and words as I went and the other voices were singing right along with me while putting in all these little moves in their melodies. I was kind of thinking, "That's cool, whoever that is."

Two girls from Puerto Rico who had backgrounds in witchcraft came to the revival that night. When I started singing this song, hundreds of people were still being prayed for at the altars, and it is normally pretty loud. When I started to sing, "Ha—ha—hallelujah..." accompanied only by the keyboard, everything became totally quiet. The song (with the heavenly voices) was so impressive that everyone stopped to listen. This went on for probably two or three minutes. (Everybody I questioned that night heard it.)

When I stopped singing, one of the Puerto Rican girls sitting to my far right released a blood-curdling scream and I thought, *How rude of you to interrupt.* But it was almost as though a demon had left. The girl told one of the intercessors who was working with her that she had tried to get deliverance from the witchcraft that she had practiced for years, and she'd never been really free of it. Once the angels started singing, that demon left her, and that was that.

It Comes Full Circle

Once I allowed my insecurities and religious pride to be broken, God began to speak into my life again through prophecy. A prophet named Michael Ratcliff prophesied in the revival in 1995 that the Lord was giving me an anointing of "imperialism." At the beginning of the prophecy he said that I had laid down the anointing to speak the Word because I felt it was inappropriate, but that God was commanding me to open my mouth, and that I would be used as a spearhead to pierce the darkness.

He said that when I or my music went to Taiwan or mainland China, God would give me eight different currencies to work with, and that He would begin to bless me financially. I was to give and be free with it, and the people would be touched, as well as the officials.

He also said God would give me a song that would be sung around the world, and that the Lord was giving me a ministry to heal marriages. The song would be about the Lord and His love for the union of marriage. Some of the marriages healed through the song would be the marriages of heads of state in many countries, and I would sing and speak the Word of the Lord to them.

Ruth Heflin prophesied early in 1996 that because I had embraced the harvest, the Lord would make my path flat. I should take no thought, and I should not worry about the things that others do, because God would provide all that I needed—houses, food, and clothing. She also said that the Lord would move me from harvest to harvest. Anywhere in the world that there is a harvest, I would have a portion of it. The Lord said that there was a generation that would follow me, though they're incomplete, but the Lord would raise them up, and they would follow.

These prophecies closed a prophetic circle in my life by fully confirming the prophecies spoken over me long ago. Some of them have come to pass already and others are in process. Since they were in full agreement with what God had already put on my heart, I embraced them with joy. From time to time I remind the Lord about His promises to me and stand on His faithfulness. As a young man not yet in his 40's, I am hardly old enough to publish an autobiography of my life, but I am obligated of the Lord to share some of the lessons I've learned along the path of obedience.

For reasons known only to God, I have catapulted to a place of national and international exposure, and I am well aware that thousands of leaders and would-be leaders are watching me. I am writing this book from the things that I know and have experienced, and I will leave other subjects to those better qualified than I. If you are a leader in the church, whether you serve as a bishop, pastor, youth pastor, or minister of music, the things I am about to discuss in the next few chapters may be of vital importance to you in the days ahead. The glory of God has fallen on Brownsville Assembly of God in Pensacola, Florida, and it has also fallen in significant measure in Toronto, Ontario, and at Holy Trinity Brompton Anglican Church in London, England. At this writing, literally thousands of reports are flooding the offices of Brownsville Assembly testifying that God's glory is falling all across the globe.

I long to see God's glory touch your life too. Even more, I want His glory to permeate your personal ministry to others, no matter how or where you serve Him. This will be my focus for the remainder of this book. If you have abandoned the old landmarks that God established in your life years ago, then it is time for you to hurry back to those landmarks. Clear away the brush and debris that hide them and once again cherish the word of the Lord over your life. Protect those things that are holy and cleanse those things that are unclean.

Chapter 9

God's Will, His Call, and His Plan

I am convinced that we are on the verge of a third great awakening in America, but I also know that there are hundreds of thousands of worship leaders, psalmists, and frustrated pastors who are feeling lost right now. Until they find their place and take their positions, they will be ineffective and totally frustrated. The Gospel of John spells out the solution to the problem.

Jesus knowing that the Father had given all things into His hands, and that He was come from God, and went to God; He riseth from supper, and laid aside His garments; and took a towel, and girded Himself (John 13:3-4).

Jesus knew that His Father had already put everything He needed in His hands. He knew who He was and where He came from (most of us are still stuck on this point). Third, Jesus knew where He was going.

Verse 13 doesn't go into great detail; it simply tells us that Jesus was returning to His Father.

The Lord trusted His Father to work out the details for an event that had never taken place before in the history of the universe. We, on the other hand, have trouble trusting God to carry us through a driver's license exam or an opportunity to witness to the unsaved. We need to be like Peter and John. "Now when they saw the boldness of Peter and John, and perceived that they were unlearned and ignorant men, they marvelled; and *they took knowledge of them, that they had been with Jesus*" (Acts 4:13).

God is searching the earth for willing workers for the coming harvest. Most of us miss His voice because we are too busy catering to the "I want to be somebody important" problem in our lives rather than dealing with it.

Pastors, evangelists, music ministers, and youth pastors have imported the world's idea of personal possession and applied it to the holy things that are God's alone. Everywhere you go you hear church leaders and "wannabes" saying, "*My* ministry...*my* congregation...*my* church...*my* people...*my* gift...*my* music...*my* worship team" and "*my* authority." This "I, me, and mine" thinking doesn't belong in the Church; it is the exclusive property of a lost and sinful world. Our talk should peppered with "He, Him, and His" as we constantly acknowledge the sole Source of all good gifts and holy things.

We have even adopted the world's shallow definition of success as measured by outward criteria like money, attendees, membership, and media audience share. God's people haven't helped the situation with their shameless worship of men and their persuasive gifts and messages that tickle the ears and loosen the pocketbooks. God is saying, "Enough!"

The Key to Success

The biblical formula for success is summed up in one four-letter word that has been banned from most believers' vocabulary: *obey*. Most of us would rather make grand sacrifices and public demonstrations of our devotion than pull out this uncomfortable word.

*And Samuel said, Hath the Lord as great delight in burnt offerings and sacrifices, as in obeying the voice of the Lord? Behold, **to obey is better than sacrifice, and to hearken than the fat of rams.** For rebellion is as the sin of witchcraft, and stubbornness is as iniquity and idolatry. Because thou hast rejected the word of the Lord, He hath also rejected thee...* (1 Samuel 15:22-23).

True success comes through obedience to God (see Josh. 1:8). Saul's life in the Old Testament proves that anything other than obedience is disobedience, and that is why so many Christian people feel frustrated today. They are upset because the Lord won't tell them where to go or what to do. They don't realize that God expects them to do what they know they are to do already.

The Lord didn't tell me what to do. *I wanted to do what He wanted me to do,* and He chose to have me do what I'm doing at Brownsville. To me it wasn't an option. If I wanted to follow through with what I had in my heart, then I had to do what *the Lord* had put in my heart to do (even though it was against what I thought I wanted).

A lot of Christians are stuck on the merry-go-round of seeking God's will. It is never wrong to seek His will in sincerity, but the way to find His will is to seek *Him.* Too often we allow the merry-go-round to become a grand diversion that pulls our attention away from loving and worshiping the Lord. We're so busy seeking His will that we forget to seek Him and draw close to His heart. *That* is really God's will for us. The facts are simple. If we are close enough to hear His heart beat, then we automatically know His direction. I know it sounds too simple, but it is true nonetheless.

One time I was enjoying a meal with Rusty Goodman and my parents at Houston's Restaurant on West End Avenue in Nashville. I was looking out the window when Rusty said, "Lindell, what do you really want to do?" I said, "You know, if I had my perfect will, I'd want to live in this city, and I would like to have a little house with my studio in it. I'd also like to work in a really kicking church that had a good missions vision so I could work on this missions desire I've had ever since I was 14. That way I could produce records and work at the church at the same time. That's what I'd really like to do." I want you to know that God heard that.

God let me do everything I wanted to do, and He let me do it all by the time I was 32. It was almost eerie, because whatever I spoke He let me have. One time I said, "I want to live in California on the beach," and I did it. Sure, it was just a passing fancy, but the Lord was quietly weeding out my desires and saying, "Okay, I've given you this—you said you wanted it and I've given it to you. *Now are you ready for what I want?*" I knew all along that God wanted me for Himself and that the rest would take care of itself. It just took me 30-some years to accept the truth and obey it. I can tell you that I've never been happier or more fulfilled.

Check Your Heart

Whenever I talk with worship leaders, musicians, or pastors who are trying to find God's will for their lives, I ask them some probing questions to help them unveil the true motives and desires of their hearts.

1. If you are leading worship, *are you really called to lead worship?*

2. *Do you want to be a worshiper* or would you rather have a solo career?

3. *Are you just doing this as a stepping stone to get where you really want to be?* (This applies no matter what name tag you're wearing at the moment.)

4. *Do you really enjoy worshiping the Lord? Do you get lost in it?* (Even when there is no one to applaud or follow your lead?)

5. *Could you do the same thing for the rest of your life?*
   If you can't, the Lord probably wants to get you
   to the place where you can. He will probably
   leave you there until you are satisfied. Only
   then will He move or promote you.

You need to ask yourself, "Why am I in the ministry? Why do I worship the Lord? Do I need worship?
Am I really called of God to be or do a specific thing?
Why? How do I know? Am I doing this because my
mother or father said I should be a good preacher's
kid and follow in the family tradition, or because I
couldn't help but follow my heart into the pastoral or
music ministry?" Be honest: Were you ever *called* by
God? If you weren't called, then why are you doing it?

The visions and dreams that God gives you early in
your life will rarely come to pass immediately. Thus
these visions and dreams can become distorted after
awhile—especially if you start trying to make it happen
by helping God get His act together. The Holy Spirit
doesn't go for that. He will let you flounder around in
your own mess until you are ready to do it His way (especially if you are chosen for lifelong service in some
form of full-time ministry). He will use the process of
"getting there" as a character-building school to prepare you for the success He wants you to have.

I run into musicians all the time who obviously have
the glory of God on their lives. I know some who are
floundering because they are trying to make it happen
through their own efforts or initiative. I talked with

one musician who has everything going for him, yet nothing seems to work for him. There is no reason why he shouldn't make it in the music industry, but he always seems to be overlooked and bypassed. I told him, "You know, this is the work of the Lord in your life. Other people may think it is strange because you haven't made it with everything you have done. No matter what you do you seem to come up short. It is the Lord who has kept you down, and it is the Lord who has kept you from being known to this point. Do you know why? It is because *the Lord says you are His.*"

> For **promotion** *cometh neither from the east, nor from the west, nor from the south. But God is the judge:* **He putteth down one, and setteth up another** (Psalm 75:6-7).

When you have a singer who is so awesome yet fails so miserably, it is a freak of nature. For every person who can sing there are 1,500 out there who can't. If you are clearly gifted and able yet everything you touch crumbles, chances are that the hand of the Lord is drawing you to Himself. Make no mistake: He is a jealous lover. He's got you marked. The quicker you come around and obey, the easier it will be. Once He has your attention, He will say, "When I get your heart pure, your spirit humble, and your motivation blameless, then I will bring you what I have always wanted you to have. You will find that it is what you have always dreamed that you wanted."

I'm writing this book to tell you: *Find it in the beginning.* Don't waste your life in rebellion and selfish wandering. Once I yielded to God, I found myself doing everything I've ever wanted to do in ministry. Everything that really matters in life flows from your relationship with God. Jesus ministered for more than three years on the earth, but throughout the four Gospels, we see Him steal away to spend time alone with His Father. That relationship was the source of His power, wisdom, and discernment.

Jesus capsulated God's will for your life in Matthew 6: "But seek ye first the kingdom of God, and His righteousness; and all these things shall be added unto you" (Mt. 6:33). Choose the best thing like Mary did (see Lk. 10:38-42). Put aside worry and sit at His feet. When you get up, you will know what to do. There are certain things that you should know to do whether you have an angelic visitation or not.

Number 1: *Never claim God's glory for yourself.* He alone is worthy of all praise and honor. Don't let unlearned or unconcerned men give you praise that belongs only to God. Don't let flesh enthrone you when every knee should be bowing before Jesus Christ. He will have no flesh glory in His presence (see 1 Cor. 1:29).

Number 2: *Don't touch holy things reserved for God, and don't finger the spoils of the world.* Never take God's money or goods for yourself unless God clearly gives them to you with His blessing. Don't dabble in the forbidden goods of the world—they defile.

Number 3: *Always return to the Master to thank and worship Him for His grace, mercy, and provision.* Don't be like the nine lepers who were cleansed outwardly but remained unclean inside because they failed to praise the One who healed them. Be the one who returns to praise the Healer, and you will possess wholeness inside and out (see Lk. 17:12-19).

God uses some unique ingredients to create the "artistic types" among us. This can make such people very difficult to understand, disciple, manage, and live with. This is especially obvious in the Church, where pastors who must exhibit strengths in the areas of dependability, stability, discipline, and self-control, are expected to select, hire, and manage musician-types. The very qualities that make us excel in the arts have earned us the collective reputation of being undependable, unstable, undisciplined, and essentially out of control much of the time. The stereotype is unfair, but many musicians seem to go out of their way to earn and perpetuate it.

Pastors, Psalmists, and Musicians

A pastor friend in the Midwest whom I respect very much called me one time and described a very common problem. "Lindell, why can't I keep a music director? I go through them constantly. I keep them about a year and then they're gone! What is going on? (By the way, you wouldn't be available, would you?)"

"Well, can I speak frankly with you?" I said. "Give me your idea of this man's job description."

"Well, it's not that much," he said. "He has to direct three choirs and an orchestra, and lead worship."

Then I said, "Does he keep office hours from 9:00 to 5:00?" I knew what he was going to say before he said it: "Oh, of course. Everybody here does that."

"There's your problem," I said. "You just outlined a 17- to 18-hour-a-day job there. That's how long it takes to meet your 'IBM criteria' in the office each day and still be a musician and handle three choirs and an orchestra in the evenings and weekends."

"This would be tough enough under normal circumstances, but Pastor, I know you expect everyone to work as hard as you do. This man will be expected to keep pumping out music. Unfortunately, he doesn't have time to write his own music or to stir up his creative God-given gifts. That means you get pre-arranged canned music from the shelf. He will have to just throw the books in people's hands and say, 'Here, learn this.' "

"Pastor," I said, "it takes time and skill to do a choir arrangement. Sometimes I'll work on one choir arrangement five or six times before I find what really works. Each rearrangement takes four or five hours. A music director in a growing church like yours can easily get overwhelmed. He has to constantly search for songs that will please you and most of the congregation. Then he has to write chord charts for all the musicians and do those time-consuming vocal arrangements for the singers, plus there are the complicated string charts. Then the guy has to teach the thing to everybody, and that can take up to two weeks. I haven't even mentioned the offertories and worship leading he is responsible for in every service. Meanwhile there is the 'IBM 9-to-5 game' to keep up with."

I was determined to press home a point that isn't obvious to most pastors. "Nearly everybody else in the church office goes home at 4 o'clock or 5 o'clock to be with family. Your music director will come back (or never leave at all) so he can conduct rehearsals three to five nights a week—when nothing special is going on. He spends his 'free' nights on those tiresome vocal arrangements and music charts. If he is married, he will try to hold his marriage together somehow in the few hours a week left to him. It is difficult, because the music director, like the pastor, is expected to be in his place every weekend, on every holiday, and in each service (along with any special function requiring music). If your music director is like most, his wage would drop below the minimum wage if it were worked out by the hour."

"Pastor," I said, "No one can last long under those conditions. Be prepared to turn that job over every year, because you'll burn out the guy. Forget hiring someone who is a real musician who is genuinely creative. I know that's the kind of person you need to really give your church a defining sound through original music that reflects your pastoral ministry and God's work in the local body. He won't last a year. He will wither because he has no time to release his God-given creativity through fresh music."

After a pause, this pastor said, "Well, what do you suggest I do?"

"First of all, if you trust the guy, get rid of the office hours. Just tell him what you expect him to do in what time frame, and tell him it is up to him to deliver—whether he comes in at 7 a.m. or 1 p.m. every day. In my experience, a truly creative person will work even harder than you could ever require of them because they are results-driven. Say, 'I want you to direct the three choirs, lead worship, and direct the orchestra. I want anointed music, and I want you to have a word from the Lord and be fresh.' "

Then I said, "Pastor, if I were you, I would say to that guy, 'You know, if you want to work till 4 o'clock in the morning and sleep till noon, that's fine with me. Just have it together when it comes time for it to happen, that's all I want.' "

"Now I know that would be totally off the page for you because you are working machine," I told my friend, "but if you'll do it, you will have a happy psalmist and minister of music who will bend over backwards to produce for you." We need to realize that the gifts of a musician just don't spring to life on command all the time. Creativity—especially divine creativity—happens when it happens. Sometimes it may wake us up in the middle of the night. When the inspiration hits at midnight, creative-types will think nothing of working halfway through the night to get it out on paper or on a recording. Frankly, it's hard to pay someone to work that hard!

The Other Side of the Coin

Pastors find it hard to justify allowing music directors the freedom to come and go as they please when most staff members punch a clock and work daytime hours. It is easy to forget that a "music director tree" produces different fruit than an "administrative assistant tree" or an "associate pastor tree."

Many churches resemble a lifeless corporate machine more than the living organism described throughout the Scriptures. God worked through the unique personalities of Moses, Sarah, Joseph, Esther, Peter, James, Paul, John, and Nicodemus (to name a very few). God thrives on the diversity He created. Yet no one can be exempt from a certain accountability in their work and ministry—even Jesus held Himself accountable to God and man for His works. But He didn't seem to punch a time clock, and neither did anyone else who helped turn the world upside down for Christ. We need to hire and manage people in the church according to their gifts and abilities, rather than plug everybody into an unrealistic IBM-style factory slot.

I believe that there are at least four categories of music-oriented people in the Church, and we need all of them.

1. **The gifted musician** has creativity and ability, but may not have a call to the ministry. These people play on music teams and church orchestras, and some pursue a secular music career. If they are tapped as spiritual leaders, they tend to lead from their natural gifts rather than from God's anointing. They are happiest ministering under the leadership of an anointed and called

music director, worship leader, or psalmist. Those in secular careers need pastors just as much as accountants and nurses do.

2. **The called musician** is a soldier in God's army band. These musicians have felt the touch of God on their lives, but they need discipline and formal training to hone their gifts and make them effective. They can intuitively tap the creative flow of the Spirit and create new songs that touch the soul. They need Spirit-led leadership to reach God's best for them and the flock they serve. Some become "soldiers of renown" in the local church, and perhaps even nationally. Others become full-time singers or musicians in the Christian music industry (which is another reason they need godly counsel and pastoral covering).

3. **The music director/worship leader** clearly feels called to spiritual leadership. I believe that these musically gifted people function in the office of deacon in the church. They have delegated authority to direct a vital area of ministry in the church, and should fulfill all the requirements listed for a deacon *(diakoneo)* in First Timothy 3:10-13.

4. **The psalmist** exhibits an indefinable authority in their ministry that seems to set them apart from other musicians and worship leaders. While musicians sing, they will prophesy with

uncanny accuracy and express the deepest long-
ings of the congregation and the hidden secrets
of the Most High. The gift in true psalmists will
make room for them before leaders and congre-
gations (with or without official recognition).
The "psalmist" gift is not listed anywhere in the
New Testament, but I believe that the true
psalmist is actually a "called *doma* gift," in particular a prophet who ministers primarily (but
not exclusively) through the medium of music.
The *doma* gifts are the five leadership gifts listed
in Ephesians 4:8-12. David the Psalmist exemplified the New Covenant psalmist perfectly. He
was once a prophet, a priest, and a king—and
he was the psalmist who still influences our worship more than anyone in the Bible aside from
Jesus Christ.

As with every true *doma* gift, psalmists/prophets
have literally been given as living gifts from God to
the Church for the edification of the saints. Their
lives are not their own. A psalmist must fulfill the
requirements of an elder (*episkopos*—an overseer,
bishop, superintendent) listed by Paul in First
Timothy 3:2-7. Many psalmists play a supportive
role to others in pastoral, prophetic, or apos-
tolic roles.

God requires every believer—including musicians—
to demonstrate the character of God in their lives. The
gifts of God apart from the character of God are dan-
gerous and often untrustworthy in unstable hands.

That is why we all need to be held accountable to someone for our actions and stewardship of our gifts.

Young musicians and worship leaders need to prove themselves by submitting to any requirements that their pastor may impose. Once they have earned the pastor's trust and perhaps his friendship, then they can share their need for a more flexible schedule to better tap the anointing of God in their work at the church as musicians. Trust is earned, not given. When problems arise, and they usually will, they must always entreat their pastor as a father.

John Kilpatrick knew he could trust me. In fact, he trusted me more than I trusted myself, and it made my job easier. *I can't work with someone whom I'm not a friend with.* If I am a hireling, I'm not happy. So it was important for me to know the desires of Pastor Kilpatrick's heart. Then I made them my own. I also asked the Lord to help me identify with the people I served in the local body.

One Sunday morning just a few weeks into the revival, I stood up and said, "When you look around at this revival, you have to say it's a wonderful thing. *But does it scare you all like it scares me?*" I mentioned all of the strange street folks and outright "different" people coming to the revival, and then I said, "Somehow in my mind, as Americans we were raised to believe that the heyday of America was the 40's and 50's. Everything that we like, especially my generation and the generation after us, is from the past...because the present has very little stability."

Then I told the congregation that I like homemade quilts and fresh milk right from the cow with the thick cream on top. I told them, "I like fresh black-eyed peas and purple-hull peas picked out of the garden. I love warm bread and green beans and turnip greens and okra. I like all that old stuff, and I like Mayberry. I like Aunt Bea's apple pie." I meant what I said too. Then I told them, "Wouldn't it be nice if the world were like Mayberry? But you know it's not. A child who is born today can be in touch with the world with the touch of his finger the minute he is coherent, thanks to the Internet. If you want that old world back, it is never going to come back. So while we are here, though we all grieve over it a little bit, let's realize that *there is an incredible potential in this world to win the lost—if we don't become a museum of saints.*"

The older folks in the church suddenly realized that they could connect with that long-haired young man up there. They began to think, *This boy ain't too bad. His hair is long, but he knows his roots. He understands.* After I said this to the congregation under the unction of the Holy Spirit, I felt an invisible wall go down. Suddenly I had older ladies in the church come up to me and say, "Now don't you ever get your hair cut. We like it." Those precious saints just love on me because they know I *genuinely* love them and their generation. I can tell you that very few services or worship times go by that I don't sing something that my grandmother would know by heart, because I remember and value the power in my Pentecostal roots.

No matter who you are or what role you play in your church, you must love the sheep of God—all of them. Those are the precious ones whom the Son of God died for. That is the bottom line today, and it will always be the bottom line. Love is the dividing line between hirelings and genuine shepherds. Undershepherds (like psalmists, worship leaders, and church musicians) have to act like senior shepherds. They need to know and compassionately care for the sheep. This is God's master plan and will for every leader and minister (properly translated as "servant") in the Church. True revival burns with the fires of genuine love, compassion, and passion for the lost. True shepherds burn with the same passions as their Great Shepherd does.

Chapter 10

Ministry and the Touch of Glory

I've known the touch of glory from my childhood, but there is a difference between then and now. When I was little, I grew up with the glory of God in my life, and I took it for granted that it would always be there. I was aware of the fire of God as a boy. I felt God's glory flow through me and I knew what it could do to a body of yielded believers. I personally experienced the weight of God's tangible glory on my soul, and I knew what it was like to be lost in His consuming presence. I grew up around the fire and took its warmth and light for granted.

When I grew older and left home, I entered a desert where I lived without the warmth of the fire. I still belonged to the "order" of the fire, to be sure. I bore the name and made the claim, but my spiritual life seemed cold or tepid at best. I seemed to stumble through life with only a dim light during the darkest and coldest times. I had the glory all my life and didn't appreciate it—until I had to live without it. I know what it is like to be separated from God's fire (though not His love), and to be unable to find it. We all have to follow the footsteps of Jesus into a wilderness of trial. If we persevere, we will return filled with power and a fresh appreciation for the *abiding presence* of God's glory.

Yes, I could remember the glory from my childhood experiences, but the memories became so dim and covered over by disappointments and cynicism that I even began to question their authenticity. That was when I prayed the prayer of hunger on Overhill Drive in Nashville. I really appreciate God's glory today. I don't take His fire for granted because I know how miserable life can be without it. That's why my favorite word to describe this revival is *more*. What a wonderful word for revival.

Men Want Better Methods, God Wants Better Men

I am deeply concerned about a behavior pattern someone termed "The Five M's of Christianity." We need to keep hearing the voice of the Lord instead of taking the easy way out and building a religious machine that perpetuates itself. I don't know who first came up with "The Five M's," but I love the truth they reveal.

1. First God has a **man** (or woman). I wish sometimes He would just do things sovereignly, without the help of flawed men, but God always uses people to bring about His will on the earth. He

delights in using weak, flawed, and unqualified men (like Peter and John) to accomplish His will. That way He receives all the glory.

2. Second, He gives that man (or woman) a **message**. When people have confidence in a leader, they believe the message, they follow, and they're set on fire.

3. Third, man (rarely God) develops a **method**. The results that come from God's man proclaiming God's message can be overwhelming or intoxicating. You have to figure out how to handle the growth, the miraculous, the fame, or the needy. The first century Church did it through prayer and fasting and came up with a godly method. After that, man felt he could figure out a method on his own. Thus were born denominations, factions, and "the outward form of godliness that denies the power thereof" (see 2 Tim. 3:5). Once we cross the line from God-given Spirit-led methods, we get in trouble.

4. Fourth, we create a **machine**. A machine, by my definition, does work once performed by a living being. In the Church, the machines of men are built specifically to run with or without God. They are created to perpetuate the appearance of God's presence and can actually maintain an outward illusion for centuries—but the power of true godliness (and the glory of God's genuine presence) will never be there.

Since all of us at Brownsville Assembly of God are humans, I am continually on guard against the compulsion to build a machine (Pastor Kilpatrick and Stephen Hill are just as concerned as I am). Although the ride up is wonderful, there is always a ride down. God will raise up others, and there are seasons in the Kingdom, but God always takes us from glory to glory. When you see a thing peak out, you wonder, "Okay, what are You doing next, Lord?"

We don't want to create a machine at Brownsville. In America, we have built a machine called religion that basically runs with or without God moving upon the people. God doesn't have to heal or really save anybody—they can just go through the forms of religion. The problem is that we end up with millions of nominal "Christians" who have no personal, life-changing experience with God.

The day I cried out to God in desperation on Overhead Drive in Nashville, I realized that I had created a worship machine. I told the Lord, "I know how to lead a worship service without You even being there. I know how to manipulate people. Forgive me, Lord. I want You alone."

5. The final "M" is a **memorial**. After man's religion machine has run its course, there's nothing left to do but build a memorial to what God did

way back when. My Pentecostal brethren built a memorial to Azusa Street, and the Methodists built a memorial to the Wesley brothers. The Presbyterians memorialized John Calvin, and the Lutherans built their memorial for Martin Luther. All these things mark marvelous works of God on men, but do they also mark His conspicuous absence from our churches today?

We all need to ask ourselves a hard question: Is there any life in what we do anymore? Is God at the heart of what we do in His name, or are we merely studying what once was and will never be again? We cannot build our lives around lifeless memorials to godly men who had a message. We can remember, we can give thanks to God, but we don't have time to build shelters for men who have come and gone. The disciples made the same mistake on the mount of transfiguration, and the Father God Himself stopped them cold (see Lk. 9:28-35). He told them to focus on the living Christ. When they did that, they never lacked for a fresh message and confirming power. They turned the world upside down. That is our prayer for this revival—may it focus our eyes on the unchanging, glorious Savior instead of the passing event of a wonderful revival and great awakening. If we keep our eyes on Him, the fire will never, ever go out.

Machines to Avoid

I am troubled by the steady stream of preachers who tag along on the skirts of this revival simply because it's the latest thing going. They see some possible personal benefit in the association. These people are *opportunists* and *manipulators*. Let me tell you a secret: I am a manipulator and an opportunist by nature. I am no fool. I can see an opportunity. I don't think you can be a successful preacher without being persuasive, but there is fine line between godly persuasion and ungodly manipulation. Humility and proper motives serve as our plumb line for balance and righteousness.

I have had to fight the opportunist side of my nature, and God has been right there all along. The Lord told me that when I moved to Pensacola, it was one of the very few completely pure things I had ever done! Why? Because there appeared to be absolutely no opportunity in it for me. I wasn't being an opportunist, and I wasn't manipulative about it. I came here in obedience to the Lord, even though every fiber of my being protested that I was leaving my career and future behind. If you remember, there was no Brownsville Revival when I moved to Florida. God wanted me to come when my only reward was the reward of obedience. I thank Him for His grace and mercy in my life.

If you are a worship leader, I warn you: Don't misuse your abilities to manipulate people with emotional hype. Learn to lead them into the Lord's presence and you will never have to worry about "revving" them up. It is okay to capture attention with some upbeat music in the same way the apostle Paul captured the Greek philosophers' attention by saying, "I see that you worship the unknown god" in the Areopagus (see Acts 17:23).

Once he had their attention, Paul promptly pointed their eyes to God. Jesus did the same thing when He shouted to the massive crowd on the last and greatest day of a feast, "If any man thirst, let him come unto Me, and drink" (Jn. 7:37b).

Don't lean on the machine of tried and proven methods. Lean on the Spirit of God. Dare to trust the Lord for discernment and inspiration in every service. Work closely with those in authority and let God rule every aspect of the service. Most psalmists, worship leaders, and musicians lean on the tried and true machine of prepared song lists. I used to preach the doctrine of lists in worship seminars across the country, but since the revival began, the Lord has weaned me from the machine. Yes, we still prepare, and yes, I paid my dues by honing my craft as a musician and worship leader. I know thousands of songs and can do a fairly decent job of playing and singing them. But now I trust the Spirit of God to lead me—I haven't used a song list in nearly two years of continuous revival services. This obviously sets me up for some interesting situations, but God always comes through.

At times I will sing a song that seems way out in left field. To my mind, I don't see how the song should work, but I sense in my spirit that we need to go in that direction. One time I was right in the middle of a classic chorus I had started spontaneously when I knew I had to look up the words. I reached for my old Church of God red hymnal and turned to page 300 for the lyrics. A pastor was just laughing away because he knew that I didn't know all the words to the old hymn. I actually started off the song in the middle. So there I was struggling to sing the chorus and play the piano with the right hand while my left hand was frantically looking for the page with the lyrics. I eventually found them, but I didn't have my glasses on. That pastor laughed even harder when he saw me playing the piano with my right hand and holding the song book in my left. Sometimes you have to be willing to be a fool. I don't need to sit there for three hours rehearsing what I'm going to do. I know I have a repertoire in my mind. It's already there.

Many people don't realize that worship is not just jubilation or celebration. It is not simply adoration either. True worship (especially in revival) includes repentance, contrition, and a recognition of the awesome holy presence of the Lord—not in a worshipful way, but in an *awestruck* way. At times the Holy Spirit will tell me that we need to sing songs of repentance right in the middle of a worship service. Why? Because even the struggle to crawl into a place of obedience is worship. Jesus was worshiping the Father in the garden of Gethsemane when He struggled in prayer and sweat drops of blood. He was worshiping the Father by putting His flesh under, and allowing His will to die in favor of His Father's will.

True worship is the spiritual counterpart to holy communion at the Lord's table. It is active, two-way communication and powerful, life-changing dialogue. That dialogue isn't limited to phrases like, "I adore

You, I worship You, I bow before You, a glorious God." It also includes exchanges that say, "Now that I am in Your glory, now that I see Your glory and I feel Your touch, I sense that I am unclean. I suddenly hear Your voice saying, 'These things must go out of your life if You would please Me.'"

If a body of believers wants genuine revival to come, then they must decide to obey—no matter what the cost. This may not cause God's glory to instantly descend (because His glory comes when and if He decides), but it is an absolute requirement before it can even be expected. Real communion with God is walking with complete abandonment to self and total focus on Him every night, in every service. God has thousands of churches filled with busy Marthas, but He wants more of us to become humiliated Marys. Mary fulfilled the requirements of Psalm 51:17: "The sacrifices of God are a broken spirit: a broken and a contrite heart, O God, Thou wilt not despise." Mary wept, and did her talking through her tears. She worshiped and adored the Lord by wiping His feet with her hair. This was a little unconventional but it won her eternal recognition as a worshiper who was heard of the Lord. When Jesus talked, she listened. When He was silent, she remained silent and obedient at His feet. She didn't feel the need to keep things moving like Martha (and most worship leaders and pastors).

God began humbling and lovingly crushing the pride in me long before He brought me to Brownsville Assembly and the revival. He continues to correct and train me every week. A life lived in His glory is a life of continual learning and instruction in the Spirit. We have a saying in Pensacola, "We don't want to do anything to 'make the Dove fly.' " The Dove, of course, is the Holy Spirit. Although the Spirit is all-powerful, and He cannot be pushed out by man or devil, He can be grieved by man's sin and insensitivity. God the Holy Spirit fears no force or entity in the universe, but He refuses to bless sin or reside with anything that is unclean or unholy.

Anytime we knowingly choose to lean on our man-made machine of techniques and methods, we sin. After ministering in churches for decades, I've learned most of the techniques to move the hearts of people. But that doesn't mean it is right for me to use them. God has raised my standards, and if I fall back into manipulation, He lets me know about it. There have been times when I slipped into the old ways of a professional worship leader by singing the right song to move the people a certain way. The minute I did it, I could sense a lull, a hesitation come over the service. I thought, *Uh oh, what do I do now?* Everyone in the place with discernment could tell that the Lord had just said, "See ya." It is embarrassing. I'm stuck up there with no place to hide, thinking, *Oh no. I've been busted again. Whoops!* All you can do is say, "Sorry, Lord. I'll shut up." God is tired of man-made revivals and flesh-run church services. He isn't willing to share His people, His time, or His anointing with the antics of flesh any longer. Praise God!

Faces of Revival

Thousands of people come to the revival in Pensacola every week. I see their faces each service, and I know they desperately want a touch of God's glory in their lives. Only His presence will do for them. I see the faces of people who walk into the place for the first time. They look genuinely hungry, almost like the haunting faces of the starving children you see on TV. Their eyes seem to say, "Could this really be what I think it is? Is it really real? I'm going to be crushed if it's not." These people don't need a whole lot of convincing—when the glory falls, they drink it in and yield to the One they've longed for as long as they can remember.

Then there are the more intellectual faces that are struggling to remain neutral while hiding a desperate hope that the revival is genuine. I think these people lean toward the negative just to keep from being hurt and looking the fool. For them, the breakthrough to glory usually comes the second night. (There are a lot of pastors in this group.) The intellectuals from the liturgical churches seem to be the most open—they believe in the supernatural from a theoretical point of view, and it is only a short step to the personal experience. They don't practice the supernatural, but they'll believe in it quicker than an evangelical will. Evangelicals have been taught that they may have an emotional experience the day they are saved, but that they shouldn't expect another one. They should "just walk by faith, not by sight; faith is the substance of things hoped for, the evidence of things not seen" (see 2 Cor. 5:7; Heb. 11:1).

The hardest to convince, the faces that find it most difficult to enter into the revival, are from my camp and kin—the Pentecostals. Whoever had the "last wave" of God's glory finds it hard to accept the next wave. Usually they need to be skipped by a couple of waves before they can accept something new. For instance, it has been a long time since God moved on a liturgical church on a worldwide scale. (He is moving mightily through the Anglican Church in England right now.)

The Pentecostals are tempted to dismiss this wave of God's glory. Some may pass it off with an arrogant sneer and say, "Nothing new here—why, we were doing this 50 years ago. If it is really God, it will come through us. After all, we are the true Pentecostals. There is nothing from God that I can't get in my prayer closet at home." They honestly believe that since they saw people fall on the floor and shake and dance, it is no different from what happened to them when they were kids. But it is different.

This revival is a visitation of God on a massive scale, and it is bringing brokenness and total repentance before the Lord. God is restoring holiness to His Church worldwide. He is requiring all of us, great and small, young and old, ordained and profane, to humble ourselves anew before Him as little children. It is marked by uncompromising preaching about the cross and the shed blood of Jesus Christ.

This revival is marked by something else that I've already mentioned, but it must be said again. It is marked by God's glory, His weighty presence that overwhelms and consumes everyone in its path. His glory compels sinners to the altar and saints to fall to their faces in new depths of intercession. It makes the arrogant cry out for mercy and the broken dance with a joy they've never known before. And the glory of this revival cannot be duplicated, worked up, conjured up, or falsified.

The real thing only comes from the Almighty God who visits His people in sovereign majesty when, where, and how it pleases Him. There is no room for flesh to prance and pose and pretend to be worthy of the glory solely reserved for our holy God. Somehow, the fear of God returned to God's house when God showed up in His glory. Praise His name, it has been a long time coming.

The only people qualified to minister and share with the hungry in this revival are those who have personally tasted His glory themselves. There can be no secondhand witnesses—we have seen, tasted, and handled Him. He is here among us. See how He has changed my life!

I wrote this book for worship leaders who are trying to sell something they've never experienced and for pastors who are preaching about something they still long to see. There is no substitute for a touch of glory. It is God's pearl of great price that is worth selling all you own or count precious so that you may possess and experience it. Jesus said that even our worship should be supernatural. If God wanted machines to handle worship, He wouldn't have messed with mankind.

> *But the hour cometh, and now is, when the true worshippers shall worship the Father in spirit and in truth: for the Father seeketh such to worship Him. God is a Spirit: and they that worship Him must worship Him in spirit and in truth* (John 4:23-24).

I was thinking the other day about my anguished prayer on Overhill Drive in Nashville when I asked God to put me wherever He was working. Then Pastor Kilpatrick walked up to me right in the middle of an altar service, and he was grinning from ear to ear. He poked me and said, "Hey Lindell, do you remember what you said when you and I had dinner in Nashville? You said, 'John, I just want to be where people are being saved.' "

I looked down at the 700 people who had just responded to the altar call and Pastor Kilpatrick just had to say one more thing to me: "Well? Are you happy now?"

I pray that you will be engulfed in the glory of God and then go on to spread the fire of God everywhere you go. (Once you experience a touch of glory, you just can't help yourself.) If you haven't experienced the touch of God on your life, then consider the words of Jesus:

> *Ask, and it shall be given you; seek, and ye shall find; knock, and it shall be opened unto you* (Matthew 7:7).

If you have never received Jesus Christ as your personal Lord and Savior, then there is no better time than now. I don't care if you are a worship leader, pastor, or presiding bishop—is Jesus the Lord of your life? If you can't say "yes" with certainty, then I encourage you to pray this prayer with me right now, right where you are:

Lord Jesus, I want You to be my Lord and Savior, but I have sinned. I repent and I'm genuinely sorry for my sins and wrongs against others. Please forgive me and wash my sins away forever and make me like You. I want to serve You all the days of my life—without compromise or hesitation. In Jesus' name I pray these things, amen.

God touched my life with His glory when I was just a child, and that personal encounter with His presence made an impact that carried over to my adult life. I pray that you will abide in His presence every day of your life, and that you too will experience the life-changing touch of His glory.

Destiny Image
Revival Books

WHEN THE HEAVENS ARE BRASS
by John Kilpatrick.
Pastor John Kilpatrick wanted something more. He began to pray, but it seemed like the heavens were brass. The lessons he learned over the years helped birth a mighty revival in Brownsville Assembly of God that is sweeping through this nation and the world. The dynamic truths in this book could birth life-changing revival in your own life and ministry!
Paperback Book, 168p. ISBN 1-56043-190-3 (6" X 9") Retail $9.99

WHITE CANE RELIGION
And Other Messages From the Brownsville Revival
by Stephen Hill.
In less than two years, Evangelist Stephen Hill has won nearly 100,000 to Christ while preaching repentance, forgiveness, and the power of the blood in what has been called "The Brownsville Revival" in Pensacola, Florida. Experience the anointing of the best of this evangelist's life-changing revival messages in this dynamic book!
Paperback Book, 182p. ISBN 1-56043-186-5 Retail $8.99

PORTAL IN PENSACOLA
by Renee DeLoriea.
What is happening in Pensacola, Florida? Why are people from all over the world streaming to one church in this city? The answer is simple: *Revival!* For more than a year, Renee DeLoriea has lived in the midst of the revival at Brownsville Assembly of God. *Portal in Pensacola* is her firsthand account of this powerful move of the Spirit that is illuminating and transforming the lives of thousands!
Paperback Book, 182p. ISBN 1-56043-189-X Retail $8.99

Available at your local Christian bookstore.

Internet: http://www.reapernet.com

Prices subject to change without notice.

Destiny Image
Revival Books

THE GOD MOCKERS
And Other Messages From the Brownsville Revival
by Stephen Hill.
Hear the truth of God as few men have dared to tell it! In his usual passionate and direct manner, Evangelist Steve Hill directs people to an uncompromised Christian life of holiness. The messages in this book will burn through every hindrance that keeps you from going further in God!
Paperback Book, 182p. ISBN 1-56043-691-3 Retail $8.99

IT'S TIME
by Richard Crisco.
"We say that 'Generation X' does not know what they are searching for in life. But we are wrong. They know what they desire. We, as the Church, are the ones without a revelation of what they need." It is time to stop entertaining our youth with pizza parties and start training an army for God. Find out in this dynamic book how the Brownsville youth have exploded with revival power...affecting the surrounding schools and communities!
Paperback Book, 182p. ISBN 1-56043-690-5 Retail $8.99

LET NO ONE DECEIVE YOU
by Dr. Michael L. Brown.
No one is knowingly deceived. Everyone assumes it's "the other guy" who is off track. So when people dispute the validity of current revivals, how do you know who is right? In this book Dr. Michael Brown takes a look at current revivals and at the arguments critics are using to question their validity. After examining Scripture, historical accounts of past revivals, and the fruits of the current movements, Dr. Brown comes to a logical conclusion: God's Spirit is moving. *Let No One Deceive You!*
Paperback Book, 312p. ISBN 1-56043-693-X (6" X 9") Retail $10.99

Available at your local Christian bookstore.
Internet: http://www.reapernet.com
Prices subject to change without notice.